A Marriage Made in Heaven

CONTRAVERSIONS

Critical Studies in Jewish Literature, Culture, and Society

Daniel Boyarin and Chana Kronfeld, General Editors

A Marriage
Made in Heaven

The Sexual Politics of Hebrew and Yiddish

NAOMI SEIDMAN

University of California Press

BERKELEY   LOS ANGELES   LONDON

University of California Press
Berkeley and Los Angeles, California

University of California Press
London, England

Copyright © 1997 by The Regents of the University of California

Library of Congress Cataloging-in-Publication Data

Seidman, Naomi.
    A marriage made in heaven : the sexual politics of Hebrew and
Yiddish / Naomi Seidman.
      p. cm. — (Contraversions ; 7)
    Includes bibliographical references and index.
    ISBN 0-520-20193-0 (alk. paper)
    1. Jews—Languages. 2. Jewish women—Languages.
3. Bilingualism. 4. Languages in contact. 5. Yiddish language.
6. Hebrew language. 7. Jewish women—Books and reading.
8. Mendele Mokher Sefarim, 1835–1917—Language. 9. Baron,
Devorah, 1887–1956—Language. I. Title. II. Series.
PJ5113b.S45 1997
306.44′089′924—dc21   96-39172

Printed in the United States of America

1 2 3 4 5 6 7 8 9

The paper used in this publication meets the minimum require-
ments of American National Standard for Information Sciences—
Permanence of Paper for Printed Library Materials,
ANSI Z39.48-1984.

To the memory of my father,
Dr. Hillel Seidman זײַל זײַל זײַל *,*
Hebrew and Yiddish writer,
and chronicler of a vanished world

Contents

Acknowledgments

Among the birthplaces of this book is the National Yiddish Book Center, where a class taught by Aaron Lansky led to a discussion with Rena Fischer and Chana Pollock. At the YIVO Institute for Jewish Research Summer Program, Abraham Novershtern showed me what Yiddish literary scholarship could be. The most rewarding aspect of writing the dissertation that became this book was the privilege of working with Chana Kronfeld, who is surely one of the great critics and teachers of our day. Chana fulfilled her function of adviser with a remarkable blend of boundless enthusiasm, a critical engagement with every aspect of the work, and her insistence on teamwork, academic cooperation, and intellectual community. Robert Alter encouraged me in my own work and inspired me with his teaching, his research, and his witty and lucid prose style. Bluma Goldstein went over my manuscript with careful attention and sharp critical insight; her honesty and political engagement have demonstrated to me the possibility of combining a truly rigorous academic career with the most intensely felt personal and political concerns. Ruti Tsoffar was an engaging and supportive study partner in the first stages of my work. The writing and revision of this book occurred in the context of an intellectual friendship and partnership with Michael Gluzman and Peter Eli Gordon. I finished the dissertation and began reworking it at Stanford University, where Hans Ulrich Gumbrecht made me feel very much a part of the Department of Comparative Literature and Steven Zipperstein extended the resources of the Jewish Studies Program to me. Chava Weissler and Dorothy Bilik, important critics in the field of Yiddish and women's studies, generously answered my questions about their work and mailed me additional material. My mother, Sara Seidman, was my ideal reader, and her astute comments kept me honest.

My father's influence and support is beyond measure: the Ph.D. in history he received from a university in Warsaw before the war was of very little practical use to an immigrant refugee and survivor in New York, and he turned to (mostly Yiddish) journalism as a career—and worked at the writing trade until the last day of his life. I like to think that my own Ph.D., which draws so much on the Eastern European world from which he came, is something of a *tikkun* for an academic path diverted by catastrophe.

I wrote this book with the help of an Andrew Mellon Dissertation Fellowship, began revising it at Stanford University as an Andrew Mellon Postdoctoral Fellow in the Department of Comparative Literature, and finished it at the Pennsylvania State University, with the help of a grant from the Pennsylvania State University Institute for the Arts and Humanistic Studies for travel to Israel. There, the librarians at the Zionist Archives were particularly helpful. The distinguished sociolinguist Joshua Fishman graciously provided me with copies of the Yiddish cartoons that appear here. Pearl Noble, daughter and executor of the estate of Melech Grafstein, gave me permission to reprint the photograph of Sholem Aleichem's grave. Irena Klepfisz inspired and enlightened me, as she did a generation of feminist Yiddishists. You-Mayhem, rebbe of Torah and contact, pushed me to a lot of places I otherwise would have missed. David Biale, my new colleague at the Center for Jewish Studies of the Graduate Theological Union, has become a valuable intellectual resource and a wonderful conversational partner. I am also especially grateful to Eliyah Arnon, who tirelessly helped me get this manuscript into its final form.

John Schott was there through it all, and I could not have done it without him.

Introduction: Toward a Reading of Hebrew-Yiddish Internal Bilingualism

> Eros and language mesh at every point. Intercourse and discourse, copula and copulation, are sub-classes of the dominant fact of communication. . . . To speak and to make love is to enact a distinctive twofold universality. . . . [T]ogether they construe the grammar of being.
>
> —George Steiner, 1975

The traditional Ashkenazic community of Eastern Europe used a number of languages, including two that were Jewish: Hebrew (or *Loshn-koydesh*, the Holy Tongue) and Yiddish.[1] The terms "bilingualism" and "multilingualism" only imprecisely describe this phenomenon. Bilingualism usually refers to an individual's competence in two languages—any two. The use of Hebrew and Yiddish in Eastern Europe was shared by an entire community. If an individual is bilingual in English and French, for example, the languages will largely overlap; that is, the bilingual will know the word for a given concept or object in both languages. By contrast, the bilingualism of a community (the phenomenon sociolinguists call diglossia) typically involves relations of complementarity, symbiosis, and hierarchy; the two languages divide one linguistic terrain between themselves, as it were, so that one set of concepts derives from Hebrew and another from Yiddish.[2] The distinction between the bilingualism of an individual and the multiple language use of a community is especially important for a study that examines the gender dimension of Hebrew-Yiddish relations. The lines along which Hebrew and Yiddish split the field of language functions correspond to other social and cultural structures that organize the Ashkenazic community. In what I call the sexual-linguistic system of this community, Hebrew and Yiddish are the linguistic components of a much larger cultural framework.

Max Weinreich's 1959 essay on the "internal bilingualism" of Ashkenazic Jewry paved the way for a more precise description of Hebrew-

1

Yiddish relations than linguists had previously articulated.[3] Weinreich distinguishes two kinds of bilingualism in the Jewish community: the first, "external bilingualism," refers to a knowledge of both Yiddish and the language of a coterritorial non-Jewish population, say, Polish or Hungarian. The second, "internal bilingualism," involves the relationship of two Jewish languages within the Ashkenazic community, Hebrew and Yiddish. Weinreich describes these two languages as playing separate sociological roles.

> The two languages are differentiated, not community-wise, but functionally. . . . The distinction in function grows clear when we recall that the same rabbis who discussed Talmudic problems in Yiddish as a matter of course corresponded about these same problems, also as a matter of course, in Hebrew. Yiddish is the spoken language. . . . But Hebrew is the language for recording. Nachman Bratslaver may instruct his disciples to pray only in Yiddish, but when he tells his amanuensis to record his stories, Nathan understands what he means and records them in Hebrew as best he can.[4]

Weinreich goes on to complicate and qualify his differentiation of Hebrew and Yiddish functions through the relatively simple distinction between speech and writing, noting that, after all, the tales of Rabbi Nachman of Bratslav were often published in Hebrew-Yiddish editions (though with Nathan's Hebrew translation *above* Nachman's Yiddish original on the page!). Whatever the specific nature of this functional differentiation, though, Weinreich stresses how deeply ingrained the system is within the Eastern European dual-language culture. Switching from one language to another is "a matter of course," and Nathan the scribe "understands" what language he must use in recording Nachman's tales without needing to ask.

There is another important qualification to add to Weinreich's initial outline of Ashkenazic internal bilingualism. The languages *were* differentiated "community-wise," but Hebrew and Yiddish were the two languages of the community of traditional Eastern European Jews in the qualified sense that these two languages were both available to male Jews. Female Jews, with very few exceptions, participated in Hebrew-Yiddish bilingualism only as a conceptual system; that is, a woman would be aware of Hebrew's prestige and be able to read along in a Hebrew prayer book, but only rarely did women have access to the formal training required to understand what she was reading. Nevertheless, this study is centrally concerned with two crucial features of Weinreich's work. The first is the hierarchical and complementary structure of languages in internal bilingualism, which Weinreich carefully lays out. The second is the interrelationship between linguistic and social structures, the basis of Weinreich's study of Yiddish. As the subtitle of this book indicates, what interests me particularly about Hebrew and Yiddish are the ways in which the linguistic relationship reflects and reinforces the gender order of the dual-language community.

Among the ways to begin thinking about Hebrew-Yiddish as a sexual-linguistic system is to recognize the historical connections and psychological associations of Yiddish and women. In this respect, my research does not have to start from ground zero. In 1912, the Yiddish literary critic Shmuel Niger (pseudonym of S. Charney) published his groundbreaking essay "Yiddish Literature and the Female Reader."[5] Niger's essay traces the influence of women readers on Yiddish literature over a period of three hundred years and a range of literary genres. The late sixteenth and early seventeenth centuries saw the beginnings of what would become a flourishing literature of Yiddish religious texts, including a number of well-known translations and reworkings of the major works of the Hebrew library. Such Yiddish texts would typically open with an apologetic introduction explaining the necessity of writing in Yiddish for those who were ignorant of Hebrew, a social category often referred to in some variation of the phrase "women and simple people."[6] Weinreich records a few examples: "for women and men who are like women, that is, they are uneducated," "for men and women, lads and maidens," and "for women and men."[7]

A few authors explicitly linked Yiddish with women and reserved Hebrew for men; for example, one eighteenth-century Hebrew-Yiddish legal guidebook provides two prayers to be recited at a deathbed, one for each sex: "Men should recite the following prayer for a dying person in the Holy Tongue while women should use the Yiddish version."[8] Niger argues that the historical ties between women and Yiddish literature, which go beyond readership to include women's writing, publishing, and patronage of Yiddish texts, gave the older Yiddish literature a distinctively feminine cast. Not only are Yiddish literature and Yiddish writers seen as feminine, so is the God addressed in women's Yiddish prayers: "God, in the personal Yiddish prayers, becomes feminized, as it were. Just go into the women's section of a synagogue—they're praying to a feminine God."[9]

Niger's provocative arguments insist on the essential femininity of large parts of Yiddish literature. This characteristic even extends, as if by contagion, to male writers in Yiddish, such as the composer of the famous *Tsenerene*, the enormously popular seventeenth-century reworking of the Bible and midrashic material on the Bible for women.

> Without a doubt [Rabbi Jacob Ashkenazi] had a feminine character, otherwise he would not have been able to write his feminine book. . . . I am sure that when rabbis feared Yiddish, it was not only because of the way educated men avoid the uneducated, but also because of the opposition of the manly character to femininity, such as the feminine garrulousness of a Jacob ben Isaac of Yanov [Ashkenazi] and other writers of Yiddish religious books.[10]

In Niger's view, the femininity of Yiddish—evidenced by the "garrulousness" of Rabbi Ashkenazi's expansive text—applies not only to female speakers or readers of the language but also to Yiddish literature itself and to its male writers. The passage explains the conflict over the legitimacy of Yiddish as motivated by fear, and by a psychosexual fear, arising not so much between men and women as between two types of men—the manly and the feminine. The opposition Niger notes, after all, is between "the rabbis" and one of their own who writes in the feminine tongue. Thus Niger's stereotypical views of masculinity and femininity are both essentialistic and strangely indeterminate, floating free from their attachment to men and women respectively.

Niger does not end his essay with an investigation of the genres sometimes referred to as "women's literature," that is, works like the *Tsenerene* or the *tkhines*, the personal prayers composed for women and often by them as well. His analysis extends beyond the older religious genres to include the beginnings of secular Yiddish literature in the nineteenth century, detecting women's continuing influence even on those (nearly always male) writers who considered their didactic novels, popular romances, and adventure stories worlds apart from the premodern "women's literature."[11] For instance, Niger provocatively reads the prolific mid-nineteenth-century Enlightenment novelist Isaac Meir Dik in the light of his "feminine" literary antecedents, declaring that "despite his negative attitudes toward Yiddish feminine folk-creativity, Dik was actually the inheritor of the feminine premodern Yiddish style, the style of the *ivre-taytsh*."[12]

Niger never revised or expanded his essay, as he had planned, nor did he publish its promised sequel, "Yiddish Literature and the Folk."[13] Niger's failure to return to his own early research is unfortunate, but there is a sense in which I am grateful for the still open invitation and challenge implicit in his unfulfilled promise. For all the problems of

Niger's stereotypical and unexamined use of terms like "femininity," my debt to his work remains great: Niger's research into the history of Yiddish as a women's literature laid the groundwork for all later explorations of this history, my own included. Niger recognized the unique importance of the audience for Yiddish literature, not as an abstract "ideal reader" or as a statistical phenomenon, but as a historically specific determining force that took shape *within* as well as outside of literary texts. Niger also opened the question of the longevity of "feminine" Yiddish traditions, exploring the possibility that Yiddish literature's distinctive heritage had lingering effects. My own study not only begins with the historical period in which Niger's left off, the mid-nineteenth century, it also attempts a corrective to those of Niger's concepts that have not stood the test of time. Finally, Niger's work, even at its most inaccurate and outmoded, has a claim on our attention in its status as the fullest elaboration of the "myth of Yiddish femininity" to date.

Niger focused solely on the problem of Yiddish femininity, with little or no apparent interest in investigating what must have presented itself as the corollary to his argument about Yiddish—the "masculinity" of Hebrew. After all, Hebrew literary audiences, until relatively recently, were virtually exclusively male, while Yiddish audiences were only partially—if highly visibly—female. This study, unlike Niger's, assumes the importance of the links between Hebrew and Jewish men, a connection so ingrained and naturalized as to have become nearly invisible. To comprehend the connections between Yiddish and women, I argue that one also has to examine the connections between Hebrew and constructions of masculinity.

Studying the myths of Yiddish femininity in conjunction with Hebrew masculinity requires an attention not only to the separate histories of each language and literature but also to the cultural system in which the two languages interrelate. The "division of labor" characteristic of dual-language cultures is a linguistic phenomenon, but it is very much a sociological one as well, operating in conjunction with other social structures. In this area of my study I take Max Weinreich as my indispensable guide. Weinreich may have called his comprehensive analysis of Yiddish *The History of the Yiddish Language,* but even a quick perusal of this work demonstrates Weinreich's view of Yiddish as both culturally embedded in and shaped by its relation with Hebrew. For Weinreich, the history of Yiddish and the history of Ashkenazic Jewry turn out to be, for many centuries and in many regions, one and the same. Weinreich carefully lays out how the social and linguistic Ashkenazic orders, with their hierarchical structures, are intimately related and mutually reinforce each other. The relations between Hebrew and Yiddish, that is, often reflect and reinforce other (always negotiable and changing) polarities in what could be called the "symbolic system" of Ashkenazic Judaism. Thus correspondences can be drawn between Hebrew-Yiddish relations and such important oppositions as sacred/profane, educated/uneducated, and, as we have seen, writing/speech.[14] The primary focus of this study, however, is the partial but nonetheless powerful intersection between the always shifting polarities of the Hebrew-Yiddish system and the (equally unstable) male/female, masculine/feminine binary opposition. By linking Hebrew and Yiddish with the masculine/feminine opposition, I am connecting two historical rather than "natural" orders. A hierarchical power relation seems to be symptomatic of both Hebrew-Yiddish relations and Ashkenazic gender structures. Nevertheless, the full range of potential linguistic and sexual relations, from harmonic complementarity to violent conflict, have found their expression in the long history of the Hebrew-Yiddish sexual-linguistic system.

By insisting on the historicity of this system, I reject the proposition that Hebrew should be considered a masculine language or Yiddish a feminine one. The sexualized perceptions about Hebrew and Yiddish must be traced in large part to their respective literary audiences rather than to some quality intrinsic to the respective languages. After all, the perception that Yiddish was feminine certainly arose only after a substantial body of Yiddish literature addressed to women began to form. Thus Yiddish femininity antedates the rise of the Hebrew-Yiddish linguistic system by four or five centuries.

Nevertheless, the gendered associations of Hebrew and Yiddish are not simply or primarily a historical phenomenon. By the mid-nineteenth century, the period with which this study begins, the myth of Yiddish femininity had taken on a powerful independent existence out of all proportion to the circumstances of Yiddish literary history and general knowledge of these circumstances. As Christopher Hutton recently put it, "the myth of the 'femininity' and 'maternity' (and 'grandmaternity') of Yiddish has transcended the vicissitudes of history to become established as the dominant ideology of Yiddish."[15] Whether or not this ideology still holds is debatable, but something very like a myth of Yiddish "femininity," usually negatively valenced, was certainly ubiquitous in the mid-nineteenth century, and among people who may have had only the vaguest conception of Yiddish literary history. What began as a partial segregation of literary audiences soon became a symbolic structure that was woven into the very ideological and cultural fabric of Ashkenazic society.

The approach I take to the sexual politics of Hebrew-Yiddish is thus both historical and structural, diachronic and synchronic. The first chapter of this study introduces this double-pronged approach to the sexual politics of Hebrew-Yiddish relations, tracing the historical sexual segregation of Hebrew and Yiddish audiences as well as mapping out the symbolic structures that reinforced the correspondences between gender and language in Ashkenazic society. In the middle two chapters, I follow the gendering of Hebrew and Yiddish in the works of two bilingual writers, investigating how a communal social order is replicated in the work of individuals within it. I begin with Sholem Yankev Abramovitsh, generally considered the first modern Hebrew and Yiddish novelist. Abramovitsh's literary career begins more or less at the farthest reaches of Niger's narrative of Yiddish femininity; the chapter traces Abramovitsh's position as the writer who finally freed Yiddish from the hold of its feminine heritage. The third chapter is an analysis of the work of Dvora Baron, usually considered the first woman prose writer in modern Hebrew (like Abramovitsh, Baron also wrote in Yiddish). These two chapters should not be taken as setting up a simple dichotomy by analyzing a typical "male" and "female" example of Hebrew-Yiddish bilingualism. Abramovitsh's bilingualism was shared by his male colleagues. Baron's literary bilingualism, given her gender and the environment in which she wrote, attests to her exceptional rather than exemplary status. Nevertheless, Baron's position both inside and outside the "women's section" of the Hebrew-Yiddish order exposes the gendering of Hebrew and Yiddish as much as Abramovitsh's movement between masculine and feminine languages. In the last chapter, I analyze the repercussions of the gendering of Hebrew and Yiddish in the dissolution of the Hebrew-Yiddish symbiosis in the early years of this century; Hebraists and Yiddishists of that period waged fierce ideological battles in which the disintegrating sexual-linguistic system often appeared as subtext.

One way of describing the overall structure of this book is to view the first and last chapters as cultural "bookends," framing and contextualizing the more strictly literary analyses of the middle ones. Whereas the first and last chapters attempt a broad cultural survey of the sexual politics of Hebrew-Yiddish relations in two different periods, the method of the two central chapters is the examination of how the sexual-linguistic system operates in the work of two bilingual writers, one male and one female.

This project navigates a course through at least three disciplines—linguistics, cultural studies, and literary criticism. Because the focus and methodology are somewhat unorthodox, it may be worth describing them further. This study places at its center a linguistic phenomenon, though I use the tools of literary analysis to examine specific textual representations of the two languages. I make no pretense of presenting the development of Hebrew-Yiddish relations as a comprehensive historical narrative. My analysis of Hebrew-Yiddish cultural phenomena rests on what I hope are illuminating and serendipitously chosen texts, including jokes, cartoons, anecdotes, and a few photographs; it makes no claim to tell the whole story. In the same way, the examinations of Abramovitsh and Baron concern themselves narrowly with their participation in Hebrew-Yiddish cultural structures, reading their work as metadiscourse and commentary on their own experiences of Hebrew-Yiddish bilingualism. Of course, Abramovitsh and Baron are not the only bilingual writers whose work invites such a sexual-linguistic analysis; the larger picture of how bilingual writers in earlier or later periods perceived Hebrew-Yiddish relations is no more than barely outlined.

This study is selective in yet another way. Virtually all the bilingual writers, readers, and critics who enter this discussion were actually tri- or multilingual. Abramovitsh, for example, spoke and corresponded almost exclusively in Russian for many years of his life. Baron translated *Madame Bovary* from French into Hebrew. Uri Tsvi Greenberg, a Hebrew-Yiddish modernist poet mentioned in the fourth chapter, found his most powerful poetic influences in German expressionism. Eliezer Ben-Yehuda, whose mythical status as "the father of the Hebrew revival" is also discussed in chapter 4, met his wife when she tutored him in French, German, and Russian.[16] This ubiquitous multilingualism is undoubtedly also a part of the fabric of the Hebrew-Yiddish gender narrative.

Any project of this length is bound to record not only the course followed but also the roads glimpsed but not taken. I will only mention a few of them here. Although I kept strictly to my subject of Hebrew-Yiddish relations, parallels between my own research and those of other apparent cases of gendered bilingualism more than occasionally presented themselves. Sander Gilman's work on German-Yiddish relations, *Jewish Self-Hatred*, the subtitle of which characterizes Yiddish (within the German context) as "the secret language of the Jews," is one example. Gilman argues, for instance, that Karl Marx seems to have perceived Yiddish as a "feminine" language and German as a "masculine" one.

Language, gender and class all contributed to young Marx's image of the Jew. Yiddish-accented German, women, and the lower class merged with the image of the "peddler Jew," living off of his haggling in public places, to create the image of the Jew in Marx's early thought. The polar distinction between this image and the German-speaking, masculine, middle-class image of his father, earning his living from service, provides the model for the "bad" and the "good" Jew.[17]

Nor is Ashkenazic culture the only one in which language is, to some degree, gendered. We do not have to look far afield to find theoretical analyses of such cultures: Sandra Gilbert and Susan Gubar, in *No Man's Land*, elaborate the intersections between gender, language, and literature in Anglo-American modernism. Gilbert and Gubar argue that Anglo-American modernism was shaped by a cultural war between the sexes; on one side were men trained in the classical tradition, and on the other, significant numbers of women writers were entering the literary arena in spite of "women's historical exclusion from serious, formal training in just those classics which form the foundation of western literary and linguistic tradition."[18] The ready fit of such an analysis to Hebrew literature, in particular, should be apparent enough.

The second of the debates that this study only marginally engages involves the psychoanalytic and postpsychoanalytic investigations of language and gender. Much of this work can be traced to Jacques Lacan's placement of language, law, and authority within (the symbolic realm of) the father, a complex argument summarized under the evocative rubric "the Name of the Father."[19] Feminists have posited either alternative or supplementary theories equating language not with the symbolic authority of the father but with the body of the mother. Hélène Cixous, in direct response to the Lacanian appropriation of language for the masculine realm, presents feminine speech as a voice singing "from a time before law, before the symbolic took one's breath away and reappropriated it into language under its authority of separation."[20] Cixous clearly imagines the possibility of a feminine language as one that both precedes and resists patriarchal authority. Make no mistake. Yiddish was not the language of feminist revolution, or was so for only a brief moment at best. Yiddish femininity nearly always marked both Yiddish and women as inferior within a rigid patriarchal order that valorized both Hebrew and masculinity (although this inferior position sometimes allowed for the exercise of subversive power). Nevertheless, the case of the Hebrew-Yiddish system, in which Hebrew presents itself as the "Name of the

Father" within the family drama of language acquisition while Yiddish is even more strongly linked to maternity or grandmaternity, cannot fail to be of relevance to the psychoanalytic debate over language and gender.

Third among the debates on which this study touches is the current critical investigation of the problem of individual and authorial subjectivity. The concept of the author has been held up to critical scrutiny in recent years, and theoreticians like Michel Foucault have retained only a limited concept of authorship as a means of defining the borders of a corpus and limiting the proliferation of meanings within a particular text.[21] The case of bilingual creativity problematizes even this carefully circumscribed usage of the term "author." Is there a Yiddish Abramovitsh and a Hebrew one, or are they the "same" author? There is some evidence that bilingual writers did, in fact, wonder about these questions. Jewish literature is often seen as a belated tag-along to European trends, but I argue that the bilingualism common to the beginnings of modern Hebrew and Yiddish literature often led writers to insights that only later influenced European literature. Jewish bilingualism, from very early on, contributed to a sense of authorial subjectivity as fissured and cut off from its "natural" linguistic expression; this attitude is in sharp contrast with romantic or nationalist European conceptions of the organic ties that connect a people and its language. George Steiner, in describing his own multilingualism, has expressed the notion that multilingualism can give rise to a unique existential and political consciousness.

The lack of a single native tongue entailed a certain apartness from other French schoolchildren, a certain extraterritoriality with regard to the surrounding social, historical community. To the many-centered, the very notion of "milieu," of a singular or privileged rootedness, is suspect.[22]

Of course, Steiner's observations of the multilingual experience cannot be simply applied to the Hebrew-Yiddish case. While Steiner's knowledge of many languages was set against the background of a monolingual society (and a particularly strict one at that), Eastern European Jewish bilingualism created its own context, its own rootedness in community. Nevertheless, Steiner raises some provocative notions about the connections among multilingualism, extraterritoriality, and "many-centeredness." Eastern European Jewish multilingualism and extraterritoriality may well set nineteenth-century Hebrew and Yiddish literature in the proleptic stance of prefiguring, in more than one way, the postmodern condition.

1 Engendering Audiences
*Hebrew, Yiddish, and the
Question of Address*

> Before the Fall, man and woman may have spoken the same
> tongue, comprehending each other's meaning perfectly.
> Immediately after, speech divided them.
>
> —George Steiner, 1975

> The expression MAME-LOSHN ("mama-language") is a typical
> Yiddish compound of Slavic and Hebrew roots, connoting the
> warmth of the Jewish family, as symbolized by mama and her
> language, embracing and counteracting the father's awesome,
> learned Holy Tongue.
>
> —Benjamin Harshav, 1990

I

The gravesite of the Yiddish writer Sholem Aleichem (1859–1916) in the
Workmen's Circle Cemetery in Brooklyn is itself a complex and paradoxical text. On one hand, the ornately carved stone, with its ten-foot-
tall crenellated towers rising on each side, leaves no doubt about the importance of the life it marks (see fig. 1). On the other hand, the grave is
set "among the common Jewish workers, just ordinary folk," in accordance with the writer's will; and the stone itself bears a self-effacing
message that denies the grandeur of the monument on which it is inscribed.[1] The epitaph, written by the already widely acclaimed author
when he became seriously ill in 1905 (although he did not die until
1916), describes an ordinary, almost anonymous man, very nearly a paci-
fist Yiddish version of the "Unknown Soldier."

> Do ligt a yid, a posheter,
> Geshribn yidish-taytsh far vayber,
> Un farn prostn folk hot er—
> Geven a humorist a shrayber.
>
> Dos gantse lebn oysgelakht,
> Geshlogn mit der velt kapores.

Di gantse velt hot gut gemakht,
Un er—oy vey—geven af tsores!

Un davke demolt, ven der oylem hot
Gelakht, geklatsht un fleg zikh freyen,
Hot er gekrenkt—dos veyst nor got—
Besod, az keyner zol nit zen.

[Here lies a simple Jew,
who wrote *yidish-taytsh* for women,
and for the common people—
he was a humorist-writer.

He ridiculed all of life,
reviled the world.
The whole world made out very well,
and he—alas—had troubles.

And precisely when his audience
was laughing, applauding, and having a good time,
he was ailing—only God knows this—
In secret, so no one would see.][2]

This self-portrait in verse, for all its claim to reveal a sacred deathbed truth, is evidence of the persistence of Sholem Aleichem's impulse toward presenting himself in theatrical and folksy ways. Important to the epitaph's presentation of a stylized Yiddish writer is its mention of his equally stylized Yiddish readers, his "fictionalized audience."[3] Sholem Aleichem identifies his work with "women" and "common people," referring less to his actual contemporary readers than to a literary convention, the writer's address to this particular audience often found in certain genres of older Yiddish texts. The epitaph fictionalizes this audience in transparently anachronistic terms, resurrecting an era in which Yiddish writers did in fact address a readership conventionally referred to as "the women and the common people." The clearest marker of this anachronism is the appellation "yidish-taytsh," a name for the Yiddish language associated (along with "ivre-taytsh") with the older religious literature for women which by 1905, when the epitaph was first composed, had been out of general currency for at least a century or two. Why then did the writer, who had worked hard throughout his life to establish the legitimacy of Yiddish as a modern literary tongue, choose to identify himself with an outmoded Yiddish literary phenomenon? Why, in his epitaph, did he also eternalize a Yiddish literary audience that had only tenuous historical connections with his contemporary readers?

Sholem Aleichem's epitaph, with its multiple references to the writer's audience, must be read in the light of Yiddish literature's general preoccupation with the relation between writer and reader. Throughout Yiddish literary history, and certainly through the Haskalah (Jewish Enlightenment) era (1770–1880), the choice of Yiddish as a medium had been justified by the needs of a Yiddish-speaking collective. Shmuel Niger sees the interest in audience as central to Yiddish literary history.

Yiddish literature is unique in this one respect, that the needs of a community played the main role in its formation until recent times; [Yiddish literature emerged because of] external needs, not from the innermost impulse and burning of individuals thirsty for expression.[4]

Sholem Aleichem's epitaph dramatizes the clash between the two contradictory traditions Niger describes. In the first tradition, common in premodern and minor literatures, the focus is on the community served, with the writer remaining anonymous or receding into the background. The second tradition, ubiquitous since romanticism, views art as the product of an individual imagination "thirsty for expression," as Niger rather dramatically puts it; in this tradition, it is often the audience that is anonymous or distanced from the artist whose essentially solitary thoughts it may be allowed, as it were, to overhear.

The epitaph brings together the phenomena Niger places in different literary periods, the attention to an audience and the impulse toward self-expression. It begins by presenting the Yiddish writer as a dedicated public servant addressing an audience not so different from himself (a "simple Jew" writing for the "common people"). But the epitaph continues by admitting us into the more private realm of this only apparently simple man—revealing the complicated and alienated heart of a troubled modern poet. The very act of confession, however, implies that the writer has not yet completely abandoned the hope of reaching his audience. Aside from the two fictionalized addressees who are actually mentioned in the epitaph (women and common people and the prosperous audience whose appreciation for the writer is blind and unhelpful), the poem imagines at least two other audiences: the first is the one that, having been let in on the secret of Sholem Aleichem's suffering, can regard itself as party to a truer emotional intimacy with the now-dead writer. The transparent theatricality of this gambit, reinforced by the obvious disingenuousness of Sholem Aleichem's having written "yidish-taytsh far vayber," creates a second implied audience, the sophisticated readers who can be counted on to catch the writer's wink. This last historically self-conscious audience is at the farthest remove from the "women" and "common people" for whom Sholem Aleichem originally claims to be writing. Nevertheless, this sophisticated implied audience is dependent on the audience of plain folks the writer first mentions. Just as the alienated, modern Yiddish writer still bears some resemblance—if only an ironic one—to his predecessor, a public servant, so too does the modern Yiddish audience still bear some traces of its predecessor in the "women" and "common people."

Sholem Aleichem's inclusion of Yiddish literature's historical audience in his epitaph is not completely ironic. His will certainly demonstrates his respect for the "common people," at least. The epitaph, by contrast, emphasizes the centrality and independence of the female half of the stock phrase "for women and the common people," placing "women" before the line break and separating the word "women" from "the common people" with a comma. In short, Sholem Aleichem mustered all the syntactic techniques at the poet's disposal to draw our attention to the women he reclaims, in jest or half-seriously, as an important part of his audience.

Not very long after Sholem Aleichem composed his epitaph, Shmuel Niger, in his "Yiddish Literature and the Female Reader," emphasized that the connections between Yiddish and women must be sought in the question of audience.

Yiddish literature may well be unique among the literatures of the world in its having, until very recently, addressed itself to a female rather than male audience. . . . Jewish women were not only the readers and consumers of Yiddish books, they were also often the ones who encouraged the writers to write in Yiddish—to write, in fact, especially for them.[5]

Not only was the older Yiddish literature created *for* a collective, as Niger insists, it also created, imagined, and sustained this collective as a feature of its textual world. The female reader, for example, was inscribed in the title of what is probably the most important work in the Yiddish religious canon, the reworking of the Bible for women by Rabbi Jacob ben Isaac Ashkenazi of Yanov, first published in 1618 and reissued in dozens of editions until the present day. The title of this work, the *Tsenerene* (Go Out and See), alludes to the Song of Songs 3:11: "Go out and see King

Solomon, daughters of Jerusalem, in the wreath his mother wove for him on his wedding day, on the day of his heart's joy." The Hebrew imperative verbs "go out and see" are in the feminine plural.

Rabbi Ashkenazi chose his title well. The verse establishes a male object of beauty as its focus, but it acknowledges and invites the participation of women in this scene: the admiring crowd is entirely female, Solomon's wreath was woven by his mother, and the implicit cause of the king's joy is his bride. In its erotic invitation to the "daughters of Jerusalem," the title creates an arena for a joyous and mutually appreciative encounter between a male writer (or male text) and his female readers. The invitation to a female collective is hard to miss, since the Hebrew feminine plural imperative is a particularly rare linguistic form.

The *Tsenerene's* implicit apostrophe to women, though, is not typical of Yiddish literature. The largest proportion of premodern Yiddish literature addressed the general public, and when women were addressed, it was usually in a formulation that included men, as in the common title page dedication "for women and uneducated men." Sometimes these authors' addresses to their readers included an apologia for writing in the vernacular rather than in the Holy Tongue. Here, for example, is Moses Altshuler's introduction to his 1596 *Brantshpigl* (Burning Mirror), an early work of *muser*, or homiletic literature.

The book was written in Yiddish for women and men who are like women in not being able to learn much. So that when the Sabbath comes, they may read this and they will be able to understand what they read. For our holy books are in the sacred tongue and often include complicated exegetical arguments [*pilpul*] from the Talmud, and they are not able to understand. . . . The great masters of the Kabbalah teach us, and write, that not every human being possesses equal understanding. Thus I write this book for women and for men who cannot fundamentally read or understand the holy books in the sacred tongue.[6]

As Chava Weissler explains Altshuler's address to "women and men who are like women," the grouping serves as cover for what might otherwise seem a lamentable lack in a man, the inability to study religious texts in Hebrew as befits a Jewish male. Since "not all people are equally well endowed . . . provision has to be made for those who cannot attain the scholarly ideal."[7] Altshuler accounts for the phenomenon of uneducated men by implicit recourse to the "natural" model of gender disparity. If ignorance of the Holy Tongue, like sex, is inherent and immutable, then why deprive men illiterate in Hebrew of the benefits of Yiddish religious literature?

Weinreich has made the strongest argument for the fictional rather than statistical force of Yiddish female readership. In his analysis, women readers served Yiddish literature as a permanent source of legitimacy against those who argued against the need to translate religious texts into the vernacular. By foregrounding women, who were either prohibited or strongly dissuaded from Torah study in Hebrew, the potential scandal of men who could not read Hebrew (and they were numerous) was circumvented and Yiddish granted a legitimacy born of indisputable necessity.

Because it was stamped as a literature for women, Yiddish literature obtained status in society, although not a place of honor. Writings for the uneducated cannot possibly attain status, for they only serve temporary purposes; everyone wants to and can (albeit only theoretically) shed his ignorance. But the woman is permanent in society; hence Yiddish literature as a women's literature also attained permanence, and grew although in restricted fashion. Until the beginning of Westernization, when a new attitude toward Yiddish literature came into being, granting it full rights, the woman provided a kind of permission for Yiddish in writing. This also enabled men to enjoy this literature, although in slight embarrassment and disguise. Occasionally even distinguished scholars glanced into Yiddish books.[8]

In Weinreich's argument, the female audience for many genres of older Yiddish literature becomes a "legal fiction," providing cover for a second class of readers hiding behind the officially sanctioned one. Weinreich describes a range of male Yiddish readers, from the uneducated man who benefited from Yiddish translations written "for women" to the man hiding his enjoyment of "women's pleasures" and the scholar "glancing" into his wife's Yiddish book or urging his sons and daughters to read them constantly, as did the respected Gaon of Vilna. We might add to this list young boys in their mothers' care and the male writers themselves, some of whom wrote under female pseudonyms.[9] This variegated group, particularly the man "peeking into the women's books," has been described often enough and in similar enough terms to constitute a recognizable Yiddish literary convention, a second fictionalized audience.

A female "front" for male Yiddish readers may have been necessary, but at least by the nineteenth century it was not altogether comfortable. In Abramovitsh's famous version of this scenario, for a man to read or write Yiddish required a rather convoluted mental gymnastics.

Yiddish in my time was an empty vessel, devoid of everything but prattle, vanity and deceit written by fools using meaningless language, without any reputation, and the women and poor people would read these things without understanding what they were reading, and the rest of the people, although they knew no other language, would be embarrassed to read it and expose their ignorance in public. And if someone was tempted to look into a Yiddish text, he would laugh at it and rationalize his actions by saying, "I'm just skimming through a 'women's book,' a silly feminine thing, for the fun of it."[10]

In Abramovitsh's description, the self-respecting male reader enticed by a Yiddish book had to take a belittling stance toward its "real" readers, among whom "the women" were prominent. This peculiar split in Yiddish readership, between men and women and within the male reader himself, had important consequences for the development of Yiddish literature. Yiddish's "femininity" undeniably affected Yiddish literature. But just as important was the *male* position (concealed, transgressive, ashamed, mocking, or as defiantly proud as Sholem Aleichem) to which the myth of Yiddish femininity gave rise.

The anxieties and defenses of men who read Yiddish are well documented; we also have evidence that men who wrote Yiddish were similarly touched by the feminine associations with the language. Niger, we might recall, insists that Rabbi Jacob Ashkenazi, the writer/compiler of the *Tsenerene*, must have been "without a doubt a feminine character, otherwise he would not have been able to compile his 'woman's bible.'" Niger goes on to describe the aversion of the masculine character to femininity, the womanish garrulousness of a Jacob ben Isaac from Yanov.[11]

Whether one reads Niger as correctly diagnosing the misogyny of seventeenth-century attitudes toward Yiddish or expressing the pro-Yiddishist stance of his own time, his description of masculine responses to Yiddish is instructive. The "femininity" of Yiddish was a problem, above all, for men and masculinity. The choice between Yiddish and Hebrew, for bilingual writers or the bilingual community, often pitted "masculinity" against "femininity" within the individual man or male community, rather than men against women. This was especially true in the modern period, with the foregrounding of the notion of writing as individual expression. The compiler of the *Tsenerene* may not have given a thought to the psychosexual implications of his choice of literary medium. But for Niger, working in a period when writers worried obsessively about the choice of a literary language, these implications were all too pressing.

Abramovitsh's evocation of the Yiddish literary ambience of the mid-nineteenth century should be enough to assure us that Yiddish's connections with a female audience, whether fictional, metaphorical, or statistical, did not altogether cease with "the beginning of Westernization, when a new attitude toward Yiddish literature came into being, granting it full rights," to quote Weinreich. In fact, dating "the beginning of Westernization" proves a perplexing endeavor. Does Weinreich's turning point refer to the early nineteenth-century flowering of Yiddish Haskalah literature (the Jewish Enlightenment project to educate the masses, often through satire of their "medievalism" and ignorance of Western culture)? Is he alluding to the beginning of modern Yiddish literature, sometimes marked on the Jewish calendar as November 27, 1864, when the first installment of Abramovitsh's "The Little Person" appeared? Does Weinreich mean Sholem Aleichem's launching of the Yiddish *Folksbibliotek* series? The appearance of Yiddish literature's first full-scale modernist, Y. L. Peretz? The 1908 Tshernovits language conference, where Yiddish was officially proclaimed a national language (though not *the* national language, as some delegates wished) of the Jewish people?

How and when did Hebrew and Yiddish writers cease addressing an audience partially or symbolically segregated by gender? Weinreich's periodization raises more questions than it answers. We can immediately reject the possibility that what Weinreich means by Westernization is the importation to Eastern Europe of Enlightenment ideology from Mendelssohn's Germany, since this ideology was not accompanied by any significant new appreciation of Yiddish. In fact, there is a considerable lag between the beginnings of Eastern European Jewish Westernization and the movement to grant Yiddish "full rights." If anything, the early *maskilim* (practitioners of the Hebrew Enlightenment) were more contemptuous of Yiddish than the rabbis had been, believing, even when they wrote Yiddish themselves, that the ugly "Jargon" was no more than a temporary stepping-stone to the Jewish acquisition of "proper" languages—especially German. Indeed, the phenomenon Weinreich associates with premodern Yiddish literature, writers excusing their Yiddish work by recourse to the needs of a female audience, reappears in virtually the same form at the heart of the Westernization project. The popular and prolific Yiddish Haskalah novelist Isaac Meir Dik peppered his sensationalistic romance and adventure chapbooks and novellas with addresses to "the dear female reader" and instructions to women "to walk in the ways of righteousness." In 1861, Dik explicitly defended his choice to write Yiddish by the old argument that women were incapable of reading Hebrew. After writing a number of talmudic parodies in Hebrew, Dik explained,

I degraded the honor of my pen to recount an abundance of divers stories in yidish-taytsh, the vernacular now spoken, to our shame and sorrow, among our people dwelling in the land (Lithuania, Poland, Byelorussia). I wrote them for the benefit of the daughters of our people who have eyes only for the Yiddish [translation of the] Pentateuch, which is writ in a stumbling tongue and wherein unseemly passages can be found that should never be uttered by the mouths of pious women and maidens.[12]

As David Roskie writes, Dik did in fact find a large audience among women, not least because his storybooks, "in contrast with other Enlightenment works, did not frighten the pious readership."[13] Dik wrote two homiletic works explicitly addressed to women, both guides to Jewish laws incumbent on women. But even the books directed to a more general audience included women in their range of concerns. Roskies describes how Dik effected "a seemingly effortless transition from biblical proof-text to rabbinic commentary (Baba Bathra 60a) to bourgeois standards of sanitation" in his homiletic *Words of Righteousness* (1863). In the section on lodging, Dik writes that

a clever person ought to take care not to have a person live directly opposite, as our sages interpreted the verse "and he saw Israel dwelling tribe by tribe" [Nm. 24:2] to mean that Balaam saw that the doors of Israel's tents were not exactly facing each other, so that one could not see what was happening in the other's lodging. And if, with God's help, you really obtain a good apartment with all the amenities, which is as difficult to obtain as a good match, then it is incumbent upon the housewife to keep it clean and tidy.[14]

It was not only Dik's more obviously *maskilic* writing that involved women's issues. The adventure stories and reworkings of European romances tried to engage a female audience as it instructed it. In his rhyming introduction to the 1865 *The Women Shopkeepers, or Golde Mine the Abandoned Wife of Brod*, Dik promises that his story will be both "terrible" and morally elevating.

> This is a terrible tale that took place fifty years ago in Brod
> It is very important and very true; most excellent and very good
> Through it our women will understand
> How to run the house, treat their children and their man
> And that rouge and jewelry are mere emptiness
> And for us, the best fortune is family happiness.[15]

From the historical accounts, Dik succeeded in finding his audience, selling tens of thousands of copies of his more than two hundred titles. The evidence suggests that a significant share of Dik's statistical audience, as well as the most visible figures in the audience constructed by his texts, were women. One observer relates that "a Vilna housewife, when she went out to the market on Friday to buy vegetables and pastries for the Sabbath, did not forget to pick up something of Dik's for a few kopecks, and this was the tastiest of the Sabbath treats."[16]

Westernization, then, did not apparently free Yiddish writers from the impulse to apologize for their language choice, nor did it obviate the need for a Yiddish "women's literature," however much it transformed the goals of such texts. To complicate the problem, "modernity" swept over Jewish communities in waves, taking different forms in the lives of specific individuals widely separated in time and space. In fact, as Niger notes, many Yiddish Haskalah novelists, despite their explicit aim of educating the masses in general, still found themselves addressing a primarily female audience as late as the last few decades of the nineteenth century. Reversing the sixteenth-century project of translating Hebrew texts into Yiddish so Jewish women would not be tempted to read German literature, Yiddish literature was now used to draw Jewish women, and their husbands, toward the secular sphere. Dik, for instance, argued that it would have been pointless for him to write his maskilic fiction and brochures for men in Hebrew.

The religious man wouldn't touch my work, much less read it, since he carefully stays away from Haskalah literature. . . . Not so for my brochures written in Zhargon [Yiddish]. Your heart, my dear female reader, is free from all those twisted ideas. You take no pride in your Jewish learning or in your holy role. . . . You will share [these ideas] with your husband or bridegroom and work on him, even if he himself hasn't read them. A wise woman can affect her man's heart better than any holy or secular book.[17]

Dik's introduction suggests that nineteenth-century women continued to be the primary readers of Yiddish literature for much the same reasons they had always been—because of their exclusion from traditional Hebrew religious studies. What has changed is that this exclusion now represents a crucial feminine advantage in the broader social movement toward Westernization. Women, because of their now-blessed ignorance, are free of the "twisted ideas" that accompany the traditional Jewish education to which boys and men are subjected.[18] Something of the apparently unavoidable Yiddish apologetic remains in this address, however: Dik addresses his female readers as conduits to a male audience. While women, in Weinreich's formulation, had accorded Yiddish a permanent if diminished status by virtue of their sanctioned Hebrew illiteracy, now women were the crucial but apparently temporary means by which to reach a wider readership.

As the evidence shows, women readers were an important part not only of Yiddish readership but also of the dissemination of the "enlightened" ideas promulgated by the Yiddish Haskalah writers.[19] Women were more free than men not only to read Yiddish as opposed to Hebrew texts but also to read secular rather than religious literature. The different reading habits of men and women in nineteenth-century Eastern Europe are captured in the Yiddish writer Y. Y. Trunk's description of the two daughters of the Rabbi of Kalisch (1822–1889).

These aristocratic maidens would seat themselves near the window and read thick-paged novels in German and Polish, their eyes streaming tears as they sighed over the throbbing passions described within. From the courtyard rose the singsong voices of the boys who studied Talmud in the Beit Midrash [study hall].[20]

If Haskalah literature spelled not the end but only the beginning of the end of Yiddish's "female connection," then neither can we spot the final break in Abramovitsh's work. Abramovitsh, the "grandfather of modern Yiddish literature," was also a Yiddish writer for women in the spirit of the seventeenth-century composer of the *Tsenerene*, although he entered literary history through his secular, "modern" prose. At the height of his literary career, in 1875, Abramovitsh published a Yiddish translation of the traditional Sabbath hymns with commentaries. As he later explained in his Hebrew "Notes toward My Literary Biography," the translation was part of a larger project of reworking the existing Yiddish version of the prayer book, which addressed its female readers in its subtitle, "A Devotional Offering: For the Daughters of Israel."

I said to myself, the time has come to act for the good of our sisters, Jewish women, and for the simple people among us, to grant them a pure offering in a clear language, because they too have souls as we do, which long to see the glory of God. And if our holy forefathers could translate the Bible into the vernacular and our rabbis could appoint a translator to help the masses understand the living word of God, should we not also adopt their ways in order to grant wisdom and ethics to the people in a language they can understand? Why should we not give to our daughters and to all the masses of Israel the good gifts and secret sweetness in our prayers and in the paths of our religion rather than letting them wander in the darkness, reading empty works and mixed-up stories filled with vanity, with our eyes looking only to the few among us?! Is each of them not holy and does God not reside in each of them?[21]

Abramovitsh's explanation for this undertaking to his male colleagues, for all its resemblance to earlier Yiddish authors' dedications to their readers, bears the particular marks of his historical circumstances. While not much had changed in Ashkenazic educational practices to make Yiddish translations for women less necessary, something important had changed for the men who were the potential Hebrew-Yiddish translators that might explain why Abramovitsh's apologetic is even more fervent, more insistent than Altshuler's was. It is not only that there is more at stake for the modern male writer in his choice of literary medium than there was for his premodern precursors. For Altshuler, the "natural" differences between the sexes gave Yiddish works their stamp of unarguable necessity. For Abramovitsh—the maskilic believer that women have souls "just as we do"—the continuing necessity of addressing women in Yiddish combined with the perception that to write Yiddish was to "dishonor" one's pen to create an impassioned apologetic, a blend of social outrage and heated self-defense. Abramovitsh's special pleading is as much for himself as for the women for whom he wrote his Yiddish work.

Abramovitsh's popular and critical success with a wider Yiddish-speaking audience meant not only that Yiddish writers could expect to reach men as well as women but also that the stigma of writing in a language associated with women was becoming, for the most part, a vestigial cultural memory. Once the sting of Yiddish's feminine associations had dulled, the way was paved for the humorous reclaiming or ideological transvaluation of Yiddish's "femininity." It might be useful here to pay a final visit to Sholem Aleichem's gravestone and read again his affectionately rueful identification with yidish-taytsh and its traditional audience. The gravestone should be ample enough warning against seeking a simple solution to the question of where and when Yiddish and its female audience broke off their long-established relations: among its other double messages, Sholem Aleichem's epitaph reveals the inextricability of a proud, fearless ownership and an ironic repudiation of Yiddish literary history, the simultaneously increasing and diminishing power of Yiddish ties with its female audience.

II

Nineteenth-century writers who chose Hebrew as their literary medium, either exclusively or in addition to Yiddish, were no less caught up in the problem of audience than Yiddish writers. Hebrew writers had as strong a sense of popular mission as their Yiddish counterparts, whether they envisioned this mission as introducing the ignorant masses to Western liberal ideas, satirizing their follies, or recruiting the folk to national revival. Yiddish writers commonly had to battle between this sense of mission and their resistance to working in a denigrated medium with a lowbrow audience.[22] Nevertheless, beginning with Altshuler, who explained that he had chosen Yiddish "because I thought I would have more customers this way,"[23] Yiddish writers were unusually forthright about the economic advantages they enjoyed, commonly describing their work in terms of the bookselling (Abramovitsh) or merchandising (Sholem Aleichem) business rather than in the sublime vocabulary of artistic expression.

Hebrew writers faced perhaps a greater quandary: choosing Hebrew as a literary medium brought with it a certain status, but a Hebrew writer could find readers only within a limited circle of his peers (I use the male pronoun here advisedly). The Hebrew poet Yehuda Leyb Gordon, in his 1863 "Awake! My People," called on the sleeping Jewish masses to "become an enlightened nation."[24] Yet neither Gordon nor any of the other Hebrew writers before the revival of Hebrew as a vernacular could reasonably hope to reach more than a minuscule proportion of the Jewish population, much less create the radical social changes they strove for in their searing indictments and impassioned prophecies.

Dan Miron, in his study of the rise of Yiddish literature in the nineteenth century, compares the market possibilities for Hebrew and Yiddish works of the period.

Abraham Mapu's *Ahavat tsiyon* (Love of Zion, 1853), the most celebrated Hebrew novel of the century and an immediate "success," had sold 1200 copies by 1857. In 1858 a Hebrew adaptation of Eugène Sue's *Mystères de Paris* caused a sensation and made everybody envious of the adaptor, as 2000 copies of its first part were sold in one year. At the same time, the Yiddish fiction writer A. M. Dik (1814–1893), whose novelettes were printed at the same printer's shop as *Ahavat tsiyon* and *Mystères de Paris,* informed his readers: "One hundred thousand copies of my books have already been sold, and new orders from the booksellers arrive daily."[25]

The inherent contradictions in the relationship of the Hebrew *maskil* with the public he aspired to educate and reform were certainly apparent to those bilingual writers who chose Yiddish instead of Hebrew in order to find an audience. These contradictions were conspicuous as well for later historians who, with the acute vision of hindsight, often mocked the naive optimism of the Hebrew Enlightenment.[26] But the Hebrew writers themselves were often the most eloquent spokesmen for the absurdities of their position. During the same years in which works like Y. Y. Linetski's 1867 *The Polish Lad* sold tens of thousands of copies, Gordon's "For Whom Do I Toil?" lamented his inability to find more than a precious few Hebrew readers. Gordon's passionate and mournful love song to the shrinking Hebrew audience may superficially resemble conventional Yiddish addresses to the "dear reader," but it has nothing of their easy intimacy. In phrases like "whoever you are and wherever you may be," Gordon imagines what might be called an "unreliable audience," one whose existence, even on the fictional level, is uncertain. In one stanza of the long poem, Gordon asks,

> For whom, then, do I toil, I the man [*ani hagever*],
> For the handful of remaining sons of Hebrew
> Who have not yet mocked the song of Zion?
> . . . .
> O who can foresee the future, who can tell me
> That I am not the last of Zion's poets
> And you, the last readers?![27]

Gordon's lament for the scarcity of Hebrew readers catalogs the different segments of the Jewish population who might have been expected to read Hebrew literature but nevertheless do not. He begins with his parents, who "reject knowledge" and see poetry as "heresy," and goes on to deplore the lack of interest in Hebrew of his "brothers," the fellow maskilim who encourage others to leave Hebrew "each for the language of his own land." Before turning to the next generation, who are "strangers to us from childhood," the poet addresses his "sisters," the Jewish women from whom he is cut off by the very language that should link them.

> My sisters, the daughters of Zion! Perhaps
> You will turn your hearts to my poem's conversation?
> God has graced you with a pleasant spirit
> As well as grace, taste and a warm heart within—
> But alas! you've been raised as captives of the sword
> Since "Teach your daughter Torah, and she will learn folly!"[28]

Gordon describes Jewish women as "captives of the sword," a term for Jews raised outside the Jewish community (forced child conscripts in the Czarist army, for example) and thus exempt from Jewish legal obligations. These women are not educated in religious texts in the Holy Tongue, as the poet notes, because of the talmudic injunction quoted in the last line of the citation.

In "The Tip of the Yod," a poem that could well be called his feminist manifesto, Gordon also addresses "the Hebrew woman" as reader, but only to establish the fictionality of his address, for there is no woman who can hear his Hebrew words.

> Hebrew woman, who knows your life?
> You came in darkness and in darkness you will depart;
> Your sorrow and joys, your dream and desire
> Will be born within you and end inside of you.
> . . . .
>
> It is well that you do not know your fathers' tongue,
> That the house of God is locked before you,
> Since now you will not hear those who despise you
> Blessing each day the One "who did not make them a woman."[29]

Gordon calls Jewish men to task for despising Jewish women, for locking the house of God against them, for holding them "captives of the sword." But these poems also thematize the linguistic gap that separates women from the realm of masculine discourse. The "fathers' tongue" is not only off-limits to women, it is also the place where sexual hierarchy is celebrated and enforced. As Gordon bitterly puts it, if women could understand the Hebrew in which the Creator and men communicate with each other, they would experience discomfort and pain. Yet the very Hebrew words in which Gordon decries his inability to bridge the worlds of Jewish men and Jewish women widened the gap that divides them. When Gordon laments that "you've been raised as captives of the sword / Since 'Teach your daughter Torah, and she will learn folly!' " he employs a characteristic literary device of the Hebrew Haskalah, cleverly juxtaposing learned quotations. And although "The Tip of the Yod" begins by addressing the masses of Jewish women, the title is a talmudic citation unrecognizable to a woman unschooled in traditional Hebrew texts.

The desire to attract women readers to Hebrew was not just a matter of increasing the Hebrew audience, or educating women in Enlightenment values. To participate fully in the European belletristic tradition meant writing heterosexually, both in content and by addressing women as well as men. As Abramovitsh is said to have commented to the critic Yosef Klausner, "a writer-artist wants to be petted by a seventeen-year-old girl; and seventeen-year-old girls who read Hebrew were non-existent then. Hebrew literature was then a literature for men alone."[30] Moreover, as Iris Parush has shown, the expansion of Hebrew audiences to include women was considered necessary for improving Hebrew as a literary language: "The desire to address women readers . . . was also the desire to alter the character, taste, and expectations of the Hebrew-reading public and to animate it with a broader range of feeling. . . . Women were considered to be more in communion with nature, to be graced from birth with feeling and aesthetic refinement. And because of their lack of education, women's thinking had not been warped by the patterns of scholastic erudition."[31]

Despite the Hebrew writers' eagerness to find women readers, female Hebrew readership appears to have remained minimal throughout the nineteenth century. Miriam Markel-Mosesson, whose Hebrew epistolary style Gordon praises and to whom he dedicated "The Tip of the Yod," is referred to by another Hebrew writer as his sole female reader.[32] It was not until the knowledge of Hebrew was separated from male educational patterns, in the next century, that Hebrew literature acquired women readers—and writers—in any significant numbers.

It would be a mistake, though, to assume that the "femininity" of Yiddish finds more than an approximate corollary in Hebrew's "masculinity." While Hebrew study was, in fact, a nearly exclusively masculine domain, it is not easy to discern a conscious ideological articulation or cultural mythologizing of Hebrew "masculinity," certainly not before the rise of Zionism. Hebrew's associations with the Jewish father, with a patrilineal religious heritage, and with the masculine educational system certainly had far-reaching effects on the development of modern Hebrew literature; nevertheless, this "masculinity" never crystallized into an explicit or coherent ideological form. Perhaps this was because the bilingual members of the community were primarily male, while women were more strictly associated with only one of the two Ashkenazic Jewish languages. In any case, the masculine associations of Hebrew were no less powerful for being largely unremarked. Since masculinity in patriarchal structures is often conflated with the universal and the unmarked while femininity attracts ambivalent attention as the "other," the overwhelmingly masculine character of traditional Hebrew study may well have seemed less worthy of comment than the more qualified "femininity" of Yiddish readership. Thus, while both men and women spoke and read Yiddish, the "femininity" of Yiddish is a widely acknowledged cultural myth, vastly more familiar and ubiquitous than what would seem to be its truer counterpart in the "masculinity" of Hebrew. For all these reasons, Hebrew masculinity is the largely unexamined counterpart of Yiddish femininity, exposed in texts like Gordon's and Abramovitsh's but never reaching the status of popular truism.

שטאַרקע טענות מיט אַ שוואַכן שטאַנדפּונקט...

III

In 1926, a cartoonist for a New York Yiddish humor magazine wished to arouse the public's rage about what he saw as the hypocrisy of the Hebrew writers in Palestine: while these writers were protesting the state-sanctioned suppression of Hebrew in the Soviet Union, Yiddish institutions continued to be attacked in the Hebraist environment of Palestine.[33] The cartoonist made his point through the graphic shorthand of caricature, drawing a suited male figure and labeling it "Hebrew writers in Eretz Israel" (see fig. 2).[34] The man holds a sign aloft that reads, "We protest the Soviet suppression of Hebrew," seemingly heedless of the barefoot and supine woman on whose back he stands.

The cartoon's caption, "Strong complaints with a weak standpoint," works on two levels. First, it exposes the hypocrisy of the Hebraists who complain about the mistreatment of the language they hold dear while they themselves suppress Yiddish. Second, the caption cleverly suggests that the Hebrew writers not only have "strong" complaints but are also the "strong," while their standpoint is weak not only because their actions have lost them the moral high ground but also because they are standing on a weak and helpless woman.

As Joshua Fishman has commented, Yiddish cartoonists often translated verbal metaphors already circulating in Ashkenazic culture into
their pictorial equivalents to create "consensually recognizable figures"
to represent the two languages.[35] In the case of the 1926 cartoon, the
male and female figures do not conform to any specific metaphors for
Hebrew and Yiddish; nevertheless, readers could be counted on to recognize the different gender associations of the rival languages. Hebrew, as
Benjamin Harshav notes in an epigraph to this chapter, had connections
to a prestigious tradition of male religious learning. And Yiddish, its
helpmeet and workaday partner through the centuries of Ashkenazic life,
was equally connected in its speakers' minds to the maternal realm.

Religious education and scholarship were predominantly for men; schools and
study-houses were exclusively for men; teachers and preachers were male;
boys accompanied their fathers to synagogue and absorbed expressions in Hebrew and Aramaic. The Holy Tongue became associated with the male world.
Its expressions flowed into Yiddish through this channel. Yiddish books were
ostensibly printed for women though read by men as well. Yiddish was the
language of home, family events, and intimacy. It was the "mama-language,"
with all possible connotations, negative and positive, which this division implied. Subdivisions of a language into social and professional idiolects are a
general phenomenon; but here, two differently balanced idiolects—the world
of learning and the world of home and trade—met in one family.[36]

Harshav draws attention not only to gendering in the Hebrew-Yiddish
system but also to its imbrication in the Ashkenazic family structure.
The title of this book presents Hebrew and Yiddish as husband and wife,
an analogy writers used often and in various ways. But from the point of
view of the Ashkenazic child being introduced into the Hebrew-Yiddish
system, the languages were embodied in the mother and father. Thus relations between the languages could take on all the psychological complexity of a family drama; to put it otherwise, the Hebrew-Yiddish system *was* a family affair. The masculine narrative of Hebrew-Yiddish
development, as told in memoirs and historical narratives, goes roughly
like this: from his mother's presence, as well as her language, her stories, and her texts, the young male child moved to an exclusively male
world in which he was introduced to Hebrew, Aramaic, and the religious
patrilineage. While his father was, of course, present in the household
along with the mother, she was entirely missing from the educational
sphere the young boy entered when he was enrolled in school. A particular form of masculine status was acquired not automatically, on entry, but only through an arduous process of textual mastery that only a

small percentage of boys and men could hope to achieve. Failing this, the man who had not acquired a Hebrew education could expect to be subsumed in the category "men who are like women."

In much the same way that the early childhood associations of Yiddish with femininity could threaten to reappear in the life of an adult male, the strength of these associations in earlier Yiddish literature continued past the period in which they were dominant. Since Yiddish "women's" literature continued to be read for hundreds of years after it first appeared in the sixteenth and seventeenth centuries, a child being raised in a traditional bilingual home would encounter it through his or her mother early in life; thus the larger history was repeated in microcosmic form in the life of the individual, heightening the connections between the feminized childhood of the Jewish male and the feminized premodernity of Yiddish literature. Weinreich describes the family associations of Hebrew and Yiddish with the Jewish father and mother as creating more than just an intellectual connection. The psychological backdrop of Hebrew-Yiddish bilingualism, because this bilingualism was so closely linked with family, could not but be emotionally as well as sexually charged.

Because *Loshn-koydesh* is so much more associated with the male world, it is also more an acquisition of the male in the family, the father. For women the role of *Loshn-koydesh* was more marginal, although there were a considerable number of women who also knew *Loshn-koydesh*. In the case of a boy, his knowledge of *Loshn-koydesh* grows in direct proportion to his physical development. Before he leaves his mother's domain and is being carried to *kheyder*, *Loshn-koydesh* plays a minimal role in his life: the prayer *Moyde ani*, a few benedictions. The teacher was always a male. No one was ever flogged for not knowing Yiddish; the boy was examined in his studies either by his father or by a scholar. The *agode* (legendary) material was more likely derived from the mother, that is, in Yiddish, from the *Tsenerene* and the moralistic books; the father had no time. But biblical passages and *Loshn-koydesh* sayings were more likely to come from the father, and the boys accompanied their father to synagogue. We have here explicitly a long-lasting attachment of Yiddish to the mother and Hebrew to the father.[37]

Weinreich's description of Hebrew-Yiddish acquisition traces the language system to childhood development and illuminates the anxiety a male writer "regressing" to Yiddish might experience.

Hebrew-Yiddish relations may have been familial, but the family, after all, was a patriarchal one. The higher status of Hebrew in Ashkenazic bilingualism reflected and reinforced patriarchal valuations of masculine pursuits, just as the higher status of men guaranteed Hebrew's position of honor. Yiddish "femininity," for the most part, similarly reinforced the inferior status of both women and Yiddish. Power relations, though, are notoriously unstable. As the cartoon of Hebrew standing on Yiddish's back demonstrates, communities are capable of radical transvaluations: the Yiddishist movements of the early twentieth century are an example of concerted resistance to received cultural hierarchies, in this case, the hierarchical structure of traditional Hebrew-Yiddish relations. Yiddishist ideology brought with it not only a transvaluation of this system but also a critique of its assumptions, recognizing, for instance, that the position of "high culture"—embodied in the Hebrew bully of the cartoon—could be read as a reflector of institutional power rather than as a measure of objective cultural worth. Readers could be expected to recognize in the cartoon not only the gendering of the languages but also the power and class differences between the figures representing Hebrew and Yiddish: the Hebraist's suit and hat signals "bourgeois" in the Socialist Yiddishist rhetoric of the period. In the ramified metadiscourse of Hebrew-Yiddish culture in which this cartoon participates, received cultural myths are transformed to suit the new class and gender ideologies of the twentieth century.

The cartoonists who published in the Yiddish humor magazines of the early decades of the twentieth century developed codes designed to distinguish Hebrew from Yiddish even when they portray *both* languages as female figures. Thus Hebrew might appear as a woman with idealized features, stylized biblical or classical garb, and a statuesque bearing while Yiddish would be more likely to have characteristics drawn from a realist, "low culture," repertoire—an apron or a plump figure, for instance. Similarly, one of Yiddish's many names, *mame-loshn* (or "mama-language," in Harshav's translation), expresses the feminine associations of Yiddish by linking the language with a certain kind of woman, a literalized "figure of speech." While the term "mother tongue" (or *mutershprakh*, its modern sociological Yiddish equivalent) is a "dead" metaphorical abstraction used with equal ease for whatever one's first language happens to be, "mame-loshn" evokes the specific set of cultural characteristics and stereotypes associated with the Eastern European Jewish mother. Implicit in this identification is the generational dimension: Yiddish is not only the language of women, it is also the language of older rather than younger women.[38] Thus, while many languages are figured as feminine in various contexts, this figuration is more specific, less abstract, more dense in the case of Yiddish.

One cartoon that appeared in 1926 depicted Chayim Nachman

Bialik's choice of Hebrew over the Yiddish in which he composed some of his earlier verse (see fig. 3).[39] The drawing shows Bialik walking arm-in-arm with an unsmiling young woman in flowing (presumably biblical) garb, with "Hebrew" written across her headdress; Hebrew looks rather haughtily at two figures standing by the side of the road, a woman dressed in the bonnet of a servant girl with "Yiddish" written across her apron and a child, who is shouting the Yiddish word for father, "tate." Bialik, in waistcoat and tails, is the image of bourgeois respectability. The street drama is designed to create the maximum amount of sympathy for the young mother. She isn't trying to create a scene, the cartoonist implies; Yiddish holds her son back, and attempts to placate the annoyed and snobbish Hebrew. "No, It's a Legitimate [or "right"] Love Affair," the cartoon is entitled. The dialogue is provided underneath:

HEBREW: Who's that, Chayim Nachman, an illegitimate [or "left"] love?

YIDDISH: Don't get upset, madame, Chayim Nachman knows me since he was a child!

The cartoon presents visual clues to differentiate the two types of women/languages: the biblical headdress for Hebrew, the apron for Yiddish. The artist also uses wordplay to make a point about the political affiliations of the languages. When Hebrew asks the poet if Yiddish was a "linke libe," she is not only asking whether his affair was clandestine (*link* literally means "left," but also "wrong" or "seamy") but also implying that Yiddish is a leftist radical. The cartoon reminds us of the associations between Yiddish and the working classes while editorializing, in the title, on the political "correctness" of Bialik's early affection for Yiddish.

An earlier cartoon uses a similar pictorial code to describe a bilingual writer choosing Yiddish, this time, over Hebrew (see fig. 4). The drawing shows Y. L. Peretz walking away from the wealthy older woman enthroned under a banner proclaiming her "ha'isha hagevirta mares hebre'ish" (Madame [Wealthy] Lady Missus Hebrew). On the writer's arm is the barefoot, graceful young Yiddish.[40] The title of the cartoon is "Y. L. Peretz's folkstimlikher roman" (Y. L. Peretz's Popular Novel). The caption reads,

The Missus (Hebrew) says, "Woe to me that I have lived this long! To see my Peretz, who is in his sixties, going off with the servant girl!"

Peretz: The poor old thing! . . . It breaks the heart . . . she says! . . . and me? . . . My heart is breaking too . . . nevertheless she's a noblewoman . . . but my child! . . . love! . . . a young heart . . . young blood—don't take notice . . . it rages . . . fire and flame . . . torches! you are mine . . . come! we will ride in the chariots of time . . . we will spin gold and silver . . . we will build palaces of marble—come!

This cartoon shows Peretz moving from Hebrew to Yiddish, the reverse of Bialik's abandonment of Yiddish for Hebrew. The title cleverly plays with the double meaning of the Yiddish word *roman,* meaning both "novel" and "love affair." Peretz's turning to folk or popular motifs in his writing, the cartoonist implies, is equivalent to his turning from the elitism of Hebrew to a love for the Jewish folk. But while the previous cartoon was designed to elicit the reader's sympathy for the single mother, here our interest remains with the guilt-ridden older man drawn

to the "young blood" of Yiddish. Hebrew is too composed, too wealthy and established, too old and snobbish to be the object of anything other than a condescending pity. The cartoonist has some fun with Peretz's melodramatic protestations of love for his young girlfriend, but the readers are nevertheless made to feel the force of Yiddish's attractions. The cartoons, taken together, demonstrate Yiddish cartoonists' ability to deftly manipulate both varieties of linguistic "abandonment" to the advantage of Yiddish.

The metaphorical depictions of Hebrew and Yiddish as two kinds of women provided journalists with a rich vocabulary for describing not only a writer's language choice but also the Hebrew-Yiddish language wars in general. Commentators made full use of these metaphors to describe the First Yiddish Language Conference, which was held in Tshernovits in 1908. One report explained the difference between the "excited Hebraists" and the "friends of Yiddish, who responded in a cooler manner," by recourse to the language of domestic politics: "It was as if the tactful maid, conscious of her duties, did not wish to rile the hysterical Hebraist madam."[41] One delegate to the conference rhetorically urged Hebrew, "the old grandmother," to "hand over her keys to the young housemistress, her daughter or daughter-in-law."[42] Another delegate spoke of Yiddish as a wife (avoiding personifying Hebrew as a woman) and accused the Hebraists at the conference of being like a guest who advises his host that his wife is unsuitable for him. "The man has lived with his wife for many years in peace, and suddenly along comes someone and disturbs their domestic tranquility."[43] These speakers call on their audience's sense of class and domestic loyalties to argue that the connection between Yiddish speakers and their language is proper, timely, and natural.

Hebrew writers were capable of turning the same trope to opposite use. Bialik, for instance, used an image taken from this flexible metaphor (Yiddish and Hebrew = different kinds of women) in a letter to Sholem Aleichem (14 January 1904).

> You know, Sholem Aleichem, sometimes I am sorry that you don't write Hebrew. . . . The time has finally come for you to stop dallying so much with the "servant girl." At least fulfill the conjugal duties of a man toward his wife with the Lady and go to the servant girl only to satisfy your appetite. Huh, Sholem Aleichem? What do you say to that?[44]

While the Hebraist Bialik speaks of the "servant girl" as an understandably attractive choice for Sholem Aleichem, but one he should shun in favor of performing his proper duties to the "lady," the Yiddish humor magazine arouses the readers' sympathies rather for the "servant girl" who has been unfairly shunned by the Hebrew writer. What is expressed in Bialik's letter as duty properly triumphing over lust is transformed in the cartoon into bourgeois male arrogance and hypocritical respectability overcoming proper domestic and sexual responsibilities.

These bawdy extensions of the metaphor "language as woman" reflect the participation of this discourse in the European literary trope that views the (male) writer's relation with his literary medium as a heterosexual courtship of or intercourse with the female embodiment of inspiration, "poesy," or language itself. Given that bilingual Jewish writers had two female figures from which to choose a "partner," it is not surprising that the descriptions of their sexual conduct present them as preening womanizers. These figurings of the bilingual writer as womanizer make the most of traditional Jewish representations of Hebrew and Yiddish. Underlying the examples above, as readers would recognize, are the paired nicknames for the languages, *gvireh* (lady) for Hebrew and *shifche-moyd* or *dinst-moyd* (servant girl) for Yiddish. The nicknames suggest, first of all, the historical function of Yiddish as the language of translation for Hebrew (and German) texts, "serving" the higher-prestige "lady." But the connotations of service to Hebrew that originally motivated the nickname had come to represent, by the early twentieth century, Yiddish's working-class identifications. Yiddishist ideology increasingly championed its associations with the "common people," presumably including actual servant girls. Hebrew, by contrast, had stronger connections with, if not a middle class (such class distinctions are particularly problematic in a society where the husband might be part of a penniless intellectual "elite" while his wife ran a market stand and kept a tight grip on the pursestrings), then at least what Robert Alter calls "the rabbinic intelligentsia."[45] Thus connections with Hebrew or Yiddish could also be used to signal a writer's political affiliations, as in Bialik's "left" love affair, in his youth, with Yiddish.

The ways in which Hebrew-Yiddish relations conformed simultaneously to both a gender and an economic hierarchy are illuminated in a passage in Chaim Grade's *My Mother's Sabbaths*. Blumele, reading aloud to her sick husband from a popular bilingual ethical text with the Hebrew above and Yiddish below, is reminded of her work as a small produce seller.

Her small shriveled head is buried in the large, yellowing pages, which are separated into two by a black line. Above is the Loshn-koydesh, beneath is the ivre-taytsh.

This reminds Blumele of the rich produce dealer's house. On the upper floors he lives with his family in a lavishly furnished apartment. Whenever she goes up there, she has to wait in the foyer like a beggar; and she is frightened by the incomprehensible foreign language that the wholesaler's educated daughters and daughters-in-law speak among themselves. But downstairs, in the vegetable cellar together with the other market women, she feels at home; it's refreshing. Here one may haggle with the wholesaler to one's heart's content, and if he tries to bring up last year's debts, you can give him such a mouthful that he'll shut up. That's exactly, not to make a comparison, how the *Menoyras hama'or* looks to her, with the thick line in the middle of each page, the sacred tongue above the line and plain Yiddish below.[46]

In Blumele's comparison, the arrangement of the Hebrew and the Yiddish on the page is the textual equivalent of Jewish society's "Upstairs, Downstairs" divisions: up above they are speaking a foreign language that silences her, while below she can feel comfortable and in her element. Blumele experiences the "upper" floors as more important, but not in a sense that interests or attracts her; on the contrary, she has more power and feels more secure in the cellar. The language spoken on the upper floors of the dealer's home, however, is not Hebrew but rather a European language, presumably Russian. Whereas Blumele's inability to understand the upper portion of the text can be traced to her gender, her incomprehension of European languages is a function of her class: the upper floors are where the richer, more assimilated Jewish men and women congregate. The power dynamic Blumele intuits in the bilingual text, however, is not a misreading. Bilingual Hebrew-Yiddish texts graphically demonstrate their hierarchical assumptions by placing the Hebrew at the top of the page, even when the Yiddish is the original and Hebrew the translation (as in Nachman's tales).

As Grade shows, the class and gender dimensions of Yiddish-Hebrew differences cannot be easily separated. The category of women, as in "for women and men who are like women," used gender to account for differences between uneducated and educated men, differences that often corresponded to class. Thus uneducated men were quite literally "feminized" by their inclusion in an audience under a feminine rubric, just as Jewish women were "second-class citizens," whatever their worldly possessions, in a society that valued scholarship above all. Class, education, and gender are related concepts in the structure of Hebrew-Yiddish, although first gender and later class and ideology appeared as the dominant social categories in distinguishing the languages.

The overlapping and multiple associations of Yiddish with women, class, and educational level complicate any discussion of the social meaning of the language. In accounting for the designation "women's literature" for the older Yiddish literature, Weinreich rejects the simple, literal explanation for this designation, noting that Yiddish literature was in fact read by men as well as women. In place of a historical argument that women were the primary readers of this literature (an argument with which Niger, for instance, seems fairly comfortable), Weinreich suggests that the connection between Yiddish and women must be seen as one of analogy rather than identity.

The designation "women's literature" used by Max Gruenbaum for older Yiddish literature is, therefore, rather a metaphoric one. As the lot of the Jewish woman in traditional Jewish society, so was the lot of Yiddish literature. It was quite remote from a position of primacy in Jewish life. However, the blessing that derived from this handicap must not be overlooked.[47]

In describing the relationship between "Yiddish literature" and the "Jewish woman" as "metaphoric," Weinreich resolves the discrepancies between the term "women's literature" and the historical male and female readership of Yiddish texts. That is, language and gender are connected because they form part of a larger system that organizes Ashkenazic life. In this model, the partial historical connections of Hebrew to men and Yiddish to women and the metaphorical relation of language and gender (Hebrew/Yiddish = men/women) both have their place. And the model could be expanded a bit further, to the varieties of educational and class differences that characterized Ashkenazic society. Thus a man who only knew Yiddish was "like a woman" not so much because Yiddish was a "woman's language," but because linguistically he occupied the subordinate, that is, feminine, position in the symbolic hierarchy. In such a system, all manifestations of the hierarchical structure could reinforce each other, while an upset in one aspect of the system could reverberate through others. Questioning the acknowledged superiority of Hebrew over Yiddish, as the Yiddishists did, implicitly challenged both gender and class hierarchies, while a populist or feminist agenda might lead to a reassessment of traditional linguistic hierarchies. Male advocates of Yiddish had two ways of confronting its femininity: they could claim the language as truly belonging to men as well as women, as Abramovitsh did when he displayed his Hebrew-Aramaic education in his Yiddish writing; or they could address Yiddish's denigration as feminine by proudly reclaiming its feminine associations, as Sholem Aleichem did in his epitaph. In most cases, including the writings of Abramovitsh and Sholem Aleichem, male writers approached the issue of the connections of Yiddish with women in a variety of ways that shifted as their attitudes toward the language changed.

The ties between Hebrew and Yiddish and Jewish gender structures, then, underwent a series of changes and transvaluations from their roots in the seventeenth-century Yiddish "women's literature." Since the Hebrew-Yiddish/male-female system resonated with other facets of social organization (class, educational level, ideology), the gendering of Hebrew and Yiddish could and did continue for long after the traditional, sexually segregated communities that gave rise to this system had ceased to be dominant in Ashkenazic culture.

2 The Transsexual Imagination

A Reading of Sh. Y.
Abramovitsh's Bilingualism

> The artist's most essential quality is masterly execution, which is
> a kind of male gift, and especially marks off men from women,
> the begetting of one's thought on paper, in verse, or whatever the
> matter is.
>
> —Gerard Manley Hopkins, 1886

> If Grandmother had a beard, she'd be a grandfather.
>
> —Yiddish proverb

I

In the summer of 1909, the seventy-five-year-old Hebrew-Yiddish
writer Sh. Y. Abramovitsh traveled through Jewish Eastern Europe on
what David Frishman, a member of his entourage, called his "triumphal
tour."

The "triumphal tour" went from Vilna to Bialystok, from Bialystok to Warsaw and from Warsaw to Lodz. No other writer—Jew or Gentile—has ever
been accorded such honor. It was the journey of a duke. Thousands of people
waited at each train station, thousands of people jostled and pushed each
other to approach him, happy if they managed to shake his hand or even just
catch a glimpse of his face. In Lodz ten thousand people waited outside the
hotel where Abramovitsh was lodging. Ladies stood in brightly colored
dresses with bouquets in their hands. The cry was periodically heard: "Long
live Mendele! Long live the Grandfather." And when the writer appeared for
an instant in the window or on the balcony, the shouts continued without
cease. For hours the writer or any of his entourage could not leave the hotel;
it was simply too dangerous. Finally, after trying various things, we somehow
pushed our way through and got into a carriage. Suddenly, though, they recognized him, and what happened then is something I will never see again. I
was sitting with him in the carriage, and thousands of people were around
us, and they tried to lift the carriage up along with the old man inside.
At last they succeeded and the cry—"Long live Mendele! Long live the
Grandfather!"—broke out from a thousand throats. And as they were lifting
him I felt I was being lifted up as well.[1]

From all reports, by the end of his life Abramovitsh's stature reached proportions reserved for European royalty in his day and rock stars in our own. Abramovitsh was not the first modern Hebrew or Yiddish novelist; Avraham Mapu (1808–1867) is generally credited with having written the first Hebrew novel and Yisroel Aksenfeld (1787–1866) the first Yiddish one. But Abramovitsh, more than these predecessors, provided Yiddish and Hebrew literature with a representative figure, a celebrated spokesperson who could grant the literatures and their readers respectability by his association with it. When Frishman wrote that he felt that the crowd was lifting him up along with "the Grandfather," he meant something more than that he was lucky enough to share Abramovitsh's carriage. For Frishman, a young Yiddish writer, the adoration of the crowd overflowed the figure of Abramovitsh to embrace his own work, the literary "vehicle" he shared with the great man. Abramovitsh's literary successes, the visibility of his fame, the resonance of the Mendele persona by which he was increasingly known, and the translations of his works into Polish and Russian contributed to rescuing Yiddish literature and its readership from a humble past. What the crowd was celebrating, in some sense, was itself.

Abramovitsh's fame is particularly remarkable against the background of his beginnings as a Yiddish writer. His Yiddish literary career began in complete obscurity and only after he had overcome considerable ambivalence toward his medium. When Abramovitsh submitted his first Yiddish story in 1864 to the new Yiddish supplement of the Hebrew periodical *Hamelitz*, he left it unsigned for fear that a Yiddish publication would threaten his budding reputation as a Hebrew writer. It was only by virtue of the popularity of his work that the Yiddish author could come out of hiding. Previously, the conceptions of Hebrew and Yiddish derived significantly from their respective audiences. Now, the public figure of the author could represent the languages in which he wrote. With the rise of the "classic" Yiddish authors, the image of the amorphous female collective associated with Yiddish gave way to the "Zayde," the grandfather of modern Yiddish literature, as Abramovitsh was called. For all the benevolence of the Mendele persona, the grandfather was an unmistakably masculine figure, bearded, overflowing with talmudic turns of phrase, and, most important, commanding respect. The literary critic Bal Machshoves portrays this conceptual shift in his essay on Abramovitsh's contributions to Yiddish literature, juxtaposing the image of the writer as beloved grandfather to a description of the language as a disheveled grandmother.

"Jargon," as even talented poets saw the wildness of Yiddish, suddenly, with one stroke of Abramovitsh's pen, acquired the pedigree of a clear, pure language. "The old Grandma"—as the poet [Shimon] Frug once portrayed Jargon—"with a torn and wrinkled apron in a rainbow of stripes, on one foot a *chalitse* shoe, on the other a white Yom Kippur sock"—all at once transformed herself into a proper language.[2]

In Bal Machshoves's formulation, there is only a distant resemblance between the grandmother and grandfather. The grandmother is impoverished and has no family connections; her chalitse shoe attests to her being both widowed and rejected by her dead husband's brother ("chalitse" is the ceremony described in Deuteronomy 24:10 in which a childless widow whose dead husband's brother refuses to marry her "to establish a name in Israel for his brother" performs a release ceremony of unshoeing him and spitting in his face). The allusion thus presents Yiddish as both widowed and scorned—doubly bereft, that is, of a male partner. The grandfather, by contrast, provides a worthy pedigree for a generation of writers and readers eager to claim him as family.

Shmuel Niger more directly credits Abramovitsh with the sexual transformation of the language in which he worked. By providing the realm of Yiddish literature with the furnishings of proper Jewish masculinity, Abramovitsh made Yiddish safe for men.

[Abramovitsh] was the first significant writer in the folk literature who was learned in religious matters [*talmid-chokhemdiker*]. He brought into it the altar, the pulpit, practically the Holy Ark as well. The literature stopped being merely a women's synagogue with its *zogerke*, the woman reciting the prayers aloud for the other women to repeat after her.[3]

Niger and Bal Machshoves see Abramovitsh's triumph as a sexual exorcism, setting the bearded and bespectacled patriarchal figure where Grandmother Yiddish and the anonymous women's prayer leaders once held sway.[4] Nevertheless, this transfer was not a simple process. The construction of an adequate (and masculine) Yiddish authorship and a unitary and coherent bilingual Jewish authorship remained an only partially realized project in Abramovitsh's lifetime. Abramovitsh's best-known character, Mendele, in the role of a Yiddish writer, compares himself to Hebrew writers in terms of relative masculinity. In the Yiddish version of *The Travels of Benjamin the Third*, Mendele, the "compiler and editor" and apparently also the "cook" of the Yiddish book, describes his work as merely a temporary summary of Benjamin's adventures until the Hebrew writers rise to their task and do the job right.

So I said to myself: until my brothers the Hebrew writers, whose little fingers are thicker than my loins, wake from their deep sleep to transcribe the story of the travels of Benjamin from the beginning to the end for the good of all Israel, I will try to print a short version of them as a temporary measure. So I girded my loins like a man and got to work.[5]

Mendele, with mock deference, presents the Hebrew writers as sleeping giants whose little fingers are thicker than his loins but whose movements are presumably too slow and ponderous to get around to Benjamin's story for a while. The allusion is to 1 Kings 12:10–11, where the royal council advises Solomon's son to respond to Israelite complaints about high taxes with this hollow boast: "My little finger is thicker than my father's loins. My father imposed a heavy yoke on you, and I will add to your yoke; my father flogged you with whips, but I will flog you with scorpions." In choosing to reverse such a falsely grandiose comparison, Mendele simultaneously presents himself as less of a man than the Hebrew writers and casts doubt on their superior strength and virility. And his vision of the Hebrew writers as lost in a deep sleep (presumably of a two thousand-year duration) suggests that age and a royal lineage may be insufficient for contemporary literary needs, and the younger, more agile Yiddish can perform where Hebrew cannot.

Mendele's borrowing of the biblical boast also reactivates the physical dimension of the allusion. In drawing our attention to the physical connections between one-half of the comparison (the finger) and the act of writing, Mendele also invites a literal and vulgar reading of the other half of his comparison (the penis), as if the size of the male sexual organ were an important aspect of literary composition! Mendele's allusion unsettles his obsequious deference to the Hebrew writers in another way. Since the biblical word for little finger is *katan* (small one), Mendele deviously ends up calling the Hebrew writers' digits (stand-ins for penises in size) "their small ones," while apparently gazing jealously at their thickness.

In the second allusion of the passage, Mendele describes himself girding his loins like a man, comparing his literary work to battle. In this allusion, too, Mendele uses an exalted phrase from the biblical vocabulary of war ironically, suggesting that he himself is not really a man but only playing the part of one. In both allusions, Mendele implies that he and presumably other males who write or publish Yiddish are something less than proper men, although Mendele at least aspires to that condition. Abramovitsh makes an elaborate joke here about Hebrew, Yiddish, and comparative masculinity. If the Yiddish writer considers himself sexually inferior to his Hebrew "brother," as Abramovitsh seems to imply, then to choose Yiddish as a literary language is to throw one's sexual or gender identity into anxious question.

It is a sign of the new importance of authorship in Jewish literature that Abramovitsh was repeatedly implored to supply his readers and critics with autobiographical sketches. An often-quoted essay Abramovitsh contributed to Nochem Sokolov's literary lexicon twenty-five years after the appearance of his first Yiddish story explores the problem of Hebrew and Yiddish authorship in an exceptionally nuanced way. After narrating his early Hebrew literary career, Abramovitsh describes his turning to Yiddish for the sake of reaching a wider audience. In the apologetic motifs by which writers from Altshuler on defended their use of Yiddish, Abramovitsh explains the unfortunate impossibility of writing in "the Holy Tongue," since "most of [the people] don't know this language and speak Yiddish." Abramovitsh goes on to quote the famous question on the value of Hebrew writing that provides Gordon's poem with its title: "For whom do I toil?" From the abrupt shift in the sentence that follows, it becomes clear, however, that Abramovitsh is bringing Gordon's question to bear on the problem of Yiddish as well as Hebrew writing.

> The question, "For whom do I toil?" brought me no peace and caused me great confusion. The Yiddish of my time was an empty vessel, containing nothing but prattle and foolishness and deceit, written by simpletons with no style and no names and read by women and the poor who couldn't understand what they were reading, and the rest of the people, even if they didn't know another language, were embarrassed to read it lest it be made shamefully public that they were ignoramuses. And when someone was tempted to read a Yiddish book, he would laugh to himself and excuse his actions by saying: I just happen to be looking into a "women's book" for the fun of it, to see the foolishness of women whose minds are frivolous [*sheda'atan kalot*].[6]

Gordon's "For Whom Do I Toil?" like Abramovitsh's essay, addresses the predicament of Hebrew writers in the absence of any sizable Hebrew audience. But Abramovitsh, unlike Gordon, describes himself as choosing between audiences; for the bilingual writer, "For whom do I toil?" is really two vexing questions. The Hebrew writer might rephrase the question as, "How many readers can I hope to reach?" For Yiddish writers, the same question would read, "What *kind* of reader can I expect to reach?"

In Abramovitsh's description of his move to Yiddish, the difficulty of choosing a language tainted by its female audience is conflated with the choice of a language itself depicted as a debased female. Elizabeth Kloty

Beaujour has observed that bilingual writers often speak of the psychic difficulty of moving from one language to another in terms of "bigamy, adultery, or incest."[7] Abramovitsh's tracing of his course from Hebrew to Yiddish combines with his apparent fondness for sexual/linguistic metaphor to produce an astonishingly intricate inquiry into the psychosexual dynamics of language choice. In an introduction to his early Hebrew work on natural history, Abramovitsh sang the praises of Hebrew in conventional terms, personifying the language as his beloved mistress whom he adorned with his prose. In the case of his turn to Yiddish, the overdetermined "femininity" of the language produces a more ambivalent discourse. Drawing from a more ramified and physical vocabulary of sexual choice, courtship, and procreation, Abramovitsh describes his encounter with Yiddish as a tortured love affair.

The writers, who cared only about strengthening our holy language and felt no connection with our people, looked down on Yiddish and mocked her. And if one in a town or two in a tribe sometimes visited the accursed woman and wrote a few things, they kept them secret and covered them with their prayer shawl so that their nakedness should not be exposed.[8]

The passage bears only a superficial resemblance to the heterosexual romantic conventions ubiquitous in maskilic tributes to the personified Hebrew language. Invoking "all the admonitions of the writer of Proverbs against sexual relations with non-Jewish women,"[9] Abramovitsh depicts Yiddish writing as an act as solitary and shameful as visiting a prostitute. The romance between a writer-lover and the valorized, beautiful, and worthy (if shamefully neglected) Hebrew language affirms his heroism and masculinity; by contrast, there is nothing redeeming about the Yiddish writer's sordid interest in Yiddish. After the perverse Yiddish writer secretly visits that "accursed woman," he hides his manuscript (presumably the product of this unlawful union) underneath his prayer shawl—a symbol of proper male religious conduct. Niger, in describing Abramovitsh as having brought the "holy ark" of male religious studies to the Yiddish "women's section," recognizes in Abramovitsh's work the range of references and allusions available only to a learned Jewish man. What Niger celebrates as the infusion of Yiddish with Jewish scholarship becomes in Abramovitsh's essay a furtive attempt to cover the disgraceful act of writing in a "women's language" under his prayer shawl. The metaphor implies that Yiddish writers fear sexual exposure; the Yiddish manuscript is equated with the writers' nakedness—more specifically, their sex (ervatam). The scorn to which first the female readers and then the feminine personification of Yiddish are subjected reappears as the shame of the man who covers his Yiddish writing, which is also his nakedness, beneath the masculine cloak of the prayer shawl.

In the next passage, Abramovitsh widens his focus from the writer's "heterosexual" attention to Yiddish to the homosocial Hebrew literary culture in which this affair furtively develops.

My admirers, the "lovers of the Hebrew language," rebuked me for besmirching my honor and reputation by giving my power to that foreign woman. But my love for what was useful conquered my pride and I decided that, come what may, I would take pity on Yiddish, the unpitied daughter, and do something for my people.[10]

The Hebrew writers, a group of judgmental and perhaps also jealous men, fiercely resent their young companion turning to a woman—or the wrong woman. Yiddish is illegitimate because she is "foreign," presumably an allusion to the language's German roots. By contrast, the narrator calls Yiddish "Yehudit" (Judith), the one Hebrew term for Yiddish that is also a woman's name, and one that means "Jewish woman." Abramovitsh evokes the familiar biblical topos that figures the Jewish people as a woman, or, more specifically, as God's lover or bride; this topos is flexible enough to describe the sinning people of Israel as a prostitute, or the defeated people of Israel as a widow. The passage reinforces the equation of the feminized Yiddish language and Jewish people in expressing pity for Yiddish as the "unpitied daughter," a citation of Hosea's mirroring of God's relationship with Israel by marrying and "redeeming" a prostitute. Abramovitsh implicitly compares his choice of Yiddish with the prophet's love for the daughter born of his prostitute-wife as well as God's forgiveness of the sinful Jewish people. Whereas the Hebrew writers reject Yiddish as both sexually and ethnically alien, for Abramovitsh, Yiddish is the primary emblem of *Jewish* otherness, standing in for a people whose degradation is figured (here and in Hosea) as a kind of feminization.

Abramovitsh also alludes once again to Gordon in this passage. Gordon's "For Whom Do I Toil?" includes the lines "Say to Hebrew: Pitied sister / Do not mock my words, call me: Brother."[11] By declaring his love for the "unpitied daughter" Yiddish, Abramovitsh challenges the Hebraist imperative of Gordon's words. While Gordon raises the "daughter" to the status of a "sister" and leaves her previous degradation only implicit in his poem, Abramovitsh's naming of "the unpitied daughter" as the object of his love depicts a much more ambivalent sexual-linguistic choice.

The passage ends with Abramovitsh marrying Yiddish and, like an Ahasueras providing for his Esther, giving her everything she needs and having many children (or sons) with her, a series of events Miron describes as "a promiscuous affair redeemed by marriage and by orderly procreation."[12] The woman is redeemed, then, because there are children born of this union, the works that grant Abramovitsh fame and provide his "wife" with respectability.

And then I was inspired and wrote my first story—"The Little Person." . . . From that time on I longed for "Yehudit" and wedded her forever, providing her with perfumes and worthy goods and she became a fine-favored and beautiful matron and bore me many children.[13]

Abramovitsh's saga of the anxiety and shame of "consorting" with Yiddish appears to reach a satisfactory conclusion: overcoming the beloved language's degradation and the writer-lover's claustrophobic social environment, the couple are betrothed, marry, and bear many children. The passage, however, leaves the fairy-tale ending ambiguous, in fact, doubly so. In celebrating the marriage of writer and language *after* the "birth" of the first "child," Abramovitsh implies that this firstborn child is born out of wedlock to a single mother whose lover is absent; this status may be Abramovitsh's acknowledgment that his first story was published anonymously. And as if the cloud over its legal status were not enough, the title of this "bastard" child—"Dos kleyne mentshele," or, to translate faithfully the redundancy in the original, "the tiny little person"— leaves us in the dark about its gender. "Dos kleyne mentshele"—*mentshele* is the neuter diminutive form of the noun *mentsh* (which itself has multiple meanings)—is sexually equivocal, as is the curious double-gendered figure by which the text explains and expands on its sexually irresolute title.

II

Despite its ambiguously gendered title, "The Little Person" appears to break deliberately, even radically, with the Yiddish "women's literature" that preceded and accompanied it. The prolific Yiddish writer Isaac Meir Dik, whose popularity was at its height in the 1850s and 1860s, addressed his stories "virtually without exception" to his "dear female reader."[14] By contrast, Abramovitsh clearly imagines and works at creating a male audience in "The Little Person." The frame story takes us into a town rabbi's study, where Mendele the Bookseller and the most powerful men of the town are convened to hear the rabbi read the last will and testament of Itsik-Avraham, one of the richest and most corrupt men of Glupsk. The frame narrative ushers the reader directly into a political, religious, and textual sphere from which women and the uneducated—the traditional Yiddish audience—are ordinarily barred. "The Little Person" invites Yiddish readers to imagine themselves as important and educated men—a radical departure for a Yiddish audience. There is some suggestion that this masculine audience may not be so easy to find or to keep. Although Itsik-Avraham's will offers a generous bequest to the community and its writer is, after all, the most powerful man in town, he nonetheless sees fit to begin his confession with these beseeching words:

> In this letter, Rabbi, my entire life story is written. I beg you, Rabbi, to fulfill my request and do everything I ask of you. I beg a thousand pardons for wearying you with such a long letter. But in the end you will see that it is very useful.[15]

While Itsik-Avraham's imploring tone may be a sign of his newfound humility, it also serves as the larger text's solicitation of male readers, the kind who will only sit still to hear a story if assured of its usefulness. After all, if the busy rabbi and the town leaders take the time to hear Itsik-Avraham's narrative, no reader need be ashamed to do likewise.

The fictional audience assembled in the rabbi's study is exclusively male, but this group is far from an idealized vision of masculine Jewry. These distinguished men, it turns out, are more concerned with their growling stomachs and hemorrhoids than with the moral issues forced on them in the course of the story. Even Mendele, who makes his first appearance in this story, at first is frightened by the invitation to the rabbi's study: he hopes that his in-laws have not lodged a complaint against him for failing to keep to the terms of his daughter's dowry. For Mendele, who will publish and circulate the will among the communities of Eastern Europe, the story is initially of interest primarily as it concerns his pocket. But "The Little Person" also aspires to another (ideal and absent) reader, the appropriately named Gutman, designated in the will as the "good man" who can carry out Itsik-Avraham's dream of founding a proper, that is, enlightened, Jewish elementary school and a school where students might later learn a useful trade. Gutman is the hoped-for addressee of the final lines of the story, in which Mendele publicly announces that as soon as Gutman, whose whereabouts are unknown, happens upon the published story, "he should come to Glupsk, where the Rabbi is waiting for him to set up the Talmud Torah and do other good things."[16] Abramovitsh presents us with a Yiddish audience that is exclusively male but that is also of questionable moral standing. The sole reader whose character is beyond question never materializes. Thus Abramovitsh establishes a fictional male audience for his story and satirizes traditional and bourgeois Jewish men simultaneously.

The confession itself is organized around competing paradigms of masculine behavior, from the strong-arm tactics of Itsik-Avraham and his hypocritical mentor Iser Varger to the genteel poverty of the enlightened Gutman. Unlike Abramovitsh's first Hebrew belletristic work, *Learn Well*, which is subtitled *A Love Story* and which takes as its central concerns the "woman question" and the problem of arranged and early marriages, this story addresses itself almost exclusively to those Haskalah ideals that most concerned men: proper educational practices, productive labor, and responsible citizenship. These social problems are explored through Itsik-Avraham's attachment to one exploitative or ignorant teacher, boss, or mentor after another (Gutman is the sole positive example) in a series of failed or morally ambiguous father-son relationships.

The quest for Gutman and a proper model for Jewish life is only part of the narrative here. "The Little Person" tells another story as well, documenting the difficulties of formulating an authoritative masculine discourse in the "kitchen" language.[17] It is no accident, therefore, that this unsigned text is the account of a child who never knew his father, "since he died while I was still nursing."[18] The narrative, despite its focus on masculine development, takes its title and initial impetus from an episode in the young boy's relationship to his mother: in a strange incident that occurs in Itsik-Avraham's early childhood, the protagonist notices a "little person," presumably his own reflection, in his mother's eyes.

Once I was staring into my mother's eyes, which she would usually hit me for doing. When I saw that this time she wasn't bothering me I couldn't help asking: "Mama, what's the tiny little person in your eyes?" My mother smiled and answered, "The tiny little person is the soul, which is in no one's eyes, not in an animal's eyes, just in Jewish eyes." My mother's answer awakened many fresh, tremulous thoughts. From then on, the tiny little person caught my imagination. I saw it in my sleep, I dreamt I was playing with the little person, holding the little person, that I myself was the little person. In short, the little person was stuck in my mind. I so much wanted to be a little person. It's ridiculous, after all, a little person is a soul! Once I had a bright idea. When my mother bent her head to take a pot out of the oven, I suddenly ran up to her from behind and knocked her on the head with my fist so that the little person would fall out of her eyes. You can imagine the beating I got for that. Besides, I didn't have anything to eat that day, because my poor mother had broken the pot of stew with her forehead.

Another time I caught a bigger punishment. I was curious to know whether an animal also had a tiny little person. So I went over to a cow in the street and while I was staring into her eyes, she gored me with her horns and hurt me pretty badly. I still have the scar on my left cheek. All these blows didn't drive out [my curiosity] even a hair; just the opposite, they just drove the thought of the tiny little person into me even more.[19]

Clearly, Itsik-Avraham mistakes his own reflected image in the pupil of his mother's eye for a tiny creature, distinct from either his mother or himself. But by withholding a simple explanation that could lay the child's curiosity to rest, the mother sets in motion the quest that ultimately propels the narrative. The phrase "the tiny little person" becomes the site of competing interpretations, beginning with the mother's explanation that the image is the soul, the intangible property of the Jewish (or perhaps human) collective. The image, that is, strictly belongs neither to herself nor to her son, but to both of them.

Thus the image in the mother's eyes also acquires meaning in her words, just as Itsik-Avraham fails in grasping both the figure and his mother's interpretation of it. His rejection or misunderstanding of his mother's interpretation inaugurates a quest that follows "the little person" in all its linguistic, gendered permutations. Hearing the richest man in the town, Iser Varger (literally, Strangler), described as a "little person," this time meaning a "parasite" or "petty manipulator," the young Itsik-Avraham decides to attach himself to Iser to learn "the Torah" of how to become a "little person" in his own right. He becomes, in fact, Iser's "soul," which in this context signifies his "right-hand man," in another corrupt echo of his mother's words.[20]

The figure of the "little person" transcends this particular narrative, appearing also in the metadiscourse of Abramovitsh's literary production. Abramovitsh describes his work as involving the imaginary construction of a curious figure he calls "dos kleyne yidele" (the little Jew), who both represents a part of the authorial persona and has a quasi-independent existence apart from him—a male, or perhaps androgynous, muse. David Eynhorn, Abramovitsh's personal secretary, reports this literary practice in his memoiristic essay on the writer.

"*Yidele*, little Jew, what do you have to say?" [Abramovitsh] used to ask whenever he had difficulties in finding the proper Yiddish expression. "When I must have a certain Yiddish word and cannot find it," he would tell me, "then I call on my little Jew, place him in front of me, and order him to talk, until he discloses the word I am looking for."[21]

While Abramovitsh's "little Jew" has a particular knowledge of the Yiddish language helpful to the Russified intellectual who may have lost touch with the Jewish masses, it also has precedents in both Western and Jewish cultural traditions. The "homunculus," or "little person," recurs in everyday language as well as in mystical, artistic, and even scientific discourse, with various connotations. One species of this figure is commemorated in the terms by which many languages (including Hebrew and Yiddish) refer to the pupil of the eye. "The Little Person" reactivates this dead metaphor, since Itsik-Avraham becomes a student of the "little person" by first rejecting his mother's "lesson" and then pursuing the "little person" and a perverse education simultaneously.

The homunculus also has a place in Western literary tradition, which is populated by a number of mischievous little sprites (Ariel, Rumpelstiltskin, Peter Pan—who has his own homunculus in the figure of Tinkerbell) who might be said to belong to the same androgynous and preternaturally knowing literary family. In a tradition that incorporated mystical symbolism and Hebrew-Yiddish wordplay, the "little *yidele*" is also an explicitly textual figure, signifying the multivalent connections between Jewish identity and the Hebrew letter *yod* (popularly connected to the Yiddish word for Jew, *yid*) which is sometimes taken to represent the "little Jew" within the "Jew" or "dos pintele yid." This conflation of text and body moves in two directions: the Hebrew letter is shown to represent the Jewish body, especially in its male form (the yod sometimes signifies the penis as well as the hand); and the Jew becomes the earthly embodiment of what is simultaneously the smallest letter and the most sacred one, the yod.

For Abramovitsh, Yiddish writing involves the cooperation of the "author" and his "little Jew," the homunculus who mediates between the Jewish masses and the intellectual writer. In the scenario Eynhorn describes, there is no maternal figure to "give birth to" the little Jew; the textual "brainchild" emerges, like Athena, from the forehead of its creator. In "The Little Person," though, the homunculus is explicitly linked with a female figure. Itsik-Avraham longs for a small play-figure he can call his own and imagines he can see such a figure before his eyes, but the figure turns out to be permanently attached to his (and "its") mother. The mother-son violence of the "little person" narrative is a function of this wavering position: the son needs to reclaim what is, after all, "his own" image, but this image is lodged in the eyes of the mother, almost as if she is immutably and permanently pregnant with it.

The aggression of Itsik-Avraham's attempt to wrench the image from his mother's eyes is adequately explained in the novella as a continuation of the cycle of abuse and neglect that the child himself has suffered at his mother's hands. In addition, the narrative recounts the familiar enough conflict between a child's dependence on his mother and his drive toward separation and differentiation from her. This narrative, however, has a particular function as the foundational scene of Abramovitsh's first Yiddish story: the discord encoded in the "tiny little person" episode can be read as an allegory of the difficult birth of modern Yiddish literature from its "women's literature" matrix. To turn from writing in Hebrew to writing in Yiddish was dangerously to reverse the maturation process begun with the young boy's introduction to masculine discourse; while the established author characterized his shift to Yiddish as a normative heterosexual love affair, the unsure beginner might well experience Yiddish writing as an indulgent regression to the maternal realm. If "The Little Person" was to escape this regression, Abramovitsh needed to wrench his Yiddish text from the "kitchen" and from a literary arena still ringed by female spectators. Itsik-Avraham, in trying to knock his own image from his mother's eyes as she bends over the stove, is an abused child reacting in the only way he knows to the figure of authority who is most responsible for his neglect. At the same time, he may also stand in for the writer who attempts to wrench a sense of self from an overwhelmingly feminine medium and forge a Yiddish literary text in the image of the Jewish man.

In his narcissistic desire to possess "the little person" by knocking it from his mother's eyes, Itsik-Avraham demonstrates his rejection of his mother's interpretation of the image. Thus he both does and does not break the hold of his mother's eyes. And in Itsik-Avraham's encounter with the cow, the direction of this violence is reversed and the child is hurt. Both encounters attest to the "little person's" uncanny property of blurring male and female identities; in Itsik-Avraham's clash with the cow, the "little person" further demonstrates its capacity to drastically reverse gender roles: the little boy who insists on discovering whether "the little person" travels not only between people and genders but also between species is penetrated in a grotesque and transgendered rape that permanently scars him.

In the later explorations of the term, "the tiny little person" refers only to men, and its meaning is sharply opposed to the one tendered by Itsik-Avraham's mother. When Itsik-Avraham finally repudiates his sin of "being a little man," it is not to replace it with his mother's definition but rather with the ideal embodied in Gutman, that is, the nondiminutive man, the good enlightened adult male. That Gutman never in fact materializes suggests that Abramovitsh leaves the possibility of an authoritative, ethical masculine Yiddish discourse in grave question.

III

"The Little Person" can be read as both an important transitional narrative for the Hebrew-Yiddish bilingual author and as a narrative, in some sense, of this transition. Abramovitsh's 1894 story, "In the Days of the Noise" (or "In the Days of Earthquake"), is another liminal text, although in a slightly different way. After writing in Yiddish for some twenty years, Abramovitsh returned to Hebrew in 1886 with "In the Secret Place of Thunder." In this first of Abramovitsh's Hebrew texts that featured Mendele as the fictional author, the writer took his initial steps toward combining ironic biblical allusion with Aramaic phrases and a flexible, nonallusive vocabulary drawn from all the historic strata of the Hebrew language. While the 1886 "In the Secret Place of Thunder" introduced Mendele into Hebrew literature, the 1894 "In the Days of the Noise" brought Mendele into the Hebraist environment of the Zionists of Odessa; two years later, in 1896, Abramovitsh's Hebrew translations of his Yiddish stories began to appear.[22] "In the Days of the Noise" thus was written between Abramovitsh's return to Hebrew writing and the Hebrew-Yiddish self-translations that completed the revolution of his Hebrew prose style. "In the Days of the Noise" addresses the problem not only of writing Mendele's words in Hebrew but also of translating Mendele into a Hebrew cultural environment. If the mother-son narrative of "The Little Person" is Abramovitsh's allegory for turning to Yiddish, then "In the Days of the Noise" can be read as a comment on Abramovitsh's equally conflicted return to Hebrew.

"In the Days of the Noise" rewrites Abramovitsh's famous novella *The Travels of Benjamin the Third* for the conditions of the 1890s, when the idea of a pair of dreamers traveling to Palestine was no longer completely fantastic. As in *The Travels*, two men, Reb Leyb and Mendele himself, leave their wives and journey southward in an attempt at fulfilling their dreams of traveling to Zion. Parodying the internal Jewish traditions of fantastic travel narratives (analogous to the medieval romances that fueled Don Quixote's quest) and satirizing the romantic Jewish dreamers who believe the accounts of the Lost Tribes and the churning magical river Sambatyon, *The Travels* charts the distance between the fictional religious-fantasy travel stories with their messianic tendencies and the bleak historical and geographic conditions Benjamin consistently misreads.

"In the Days of the Noise" narrows the gap between the Zionist quest and Eastern European Jewish conditions, and Mendele and Reb Leyb actually meet the Odessa Zionists, who are at least theoretically in a position to grant their request. But the dream must remain unfulfilled, because neither the Zionists nor Mendele have the means of inaugurating the necessary changes demanded by the Zionist enterprise. Mendele is particularly incapable of recognizing his unsuitability for the Zionist ideal of physical labor. As in other stories, though, Mendele's ironic function is a double one: with his honesty and down-to-earth wit, he exposes the snobbery of the Odessa Zionists; at the same time, his ignorance of this world reveals the gulf between the traditional Jew and Europeanized Jewish modernity.

For all the story's historical-political scope, the plot is closer to the stuff of domestic farce. "In the Days of the Noise" generates comedy from a series of misunderstandings. The two protagonists have signed an economic friendship pact promising to share their fortunes, meager as they are. The pact between the two men markedly resembles a marriage contract, and the friends call each other "ben-zug," a term that could mean partner but whose primary designation is "spouse." Like Benjamin and Senderl in *The Travels*, the two men act very much as husband and wife: Mendele is outraged when Reb Leyb fails to come home one night, and he spies on his partner's strolls with the "matron" who is his rival.

Mendele's outrage is not just at Leyb's betrayal of their friendship; Mendele also feels that Leyb's association with a woman is improper behavior for a Jewish man, in fact, unmanly. After witnessing the changes in Reb Leyb after the intrusion of this mysterious woman, Mendele erupts into a bitter series of transsexual insults, seeing Reb Leyb as a pathetic and vain female.

Reb Leyb came in and stood next to my bed, and when he saw that I was asleep he stepped back and started tiptoeing around the room with tiny steps. Then he took off his weekday caftan and put on his Sabbath caftan, after checking it over very well. Then he smoothed his sidelocks and beard and tilted his hat this way and that way, snatching glimpses at himself in the wall mirror and from the smile on his face you could tell that he was well pleased with himself. It's possible that Reb Leyb found favor in his own eyes just like all those ugly women who are convinced, as they adorn themselves before the mirror, that they're great beauties without any equal. But to tell you the truth, I wasn't so pleased with him, and for me, his adornment was his ugliness, and watching him, the figure of the beautiful Joseph and the visage of Zlikha [Potiphar's wife] appeared in my imagination.[23]

Mendele's comparison of Reb Leyb with Joseph and Potiphar's wife invites and resists interpretation. Is Reb Leyb a narcissistic Joseph, or is he a lascivious Zlikha, stealing glances at the beautiful male figure? Is he both the voyeuristic woman and the "beautiful" love object? And if stolen glimpses make Reb Leyb (as voyeur) a woman, do they do the same to the "sleeping" Mendele? The biblical story of Joseph and Potiphar's wife, with its gender role reversals, reflects and refracts the already unsettled scene of narcissism and voyeurism between Reb Leyb and Mendele. The rift between them, then, feminizes not only the betrayer but also Mendele. In a later passage, the dejected Mendele tellingly compares the weekday gabardine Reb Leyb has left hanging on the wall to an abandoned wife.

It looked sad, the hem all muddy like a housewife's dress on Friday afternoon. Woe to the dress, for all the years she served her master faithfully, clung to him every weekday and was not separated from him until she became a rag, and now she has been traded in for another and has become a desolate abandoned wife [*agunah*]![24]

When Reb Leyb tries to apologize for his long absences, Mendele answers, "You need to apologize to your wife, not to me," but it is precisely in this denial that his anger reveals itself. He asks Reb Leyb whether he has been acting like a bachelor because he had signed a provisional divorce agreement before leaving for Odessa, as was common for husbands leaving for war or on dangerous expeditions. Reb Leyb answers that the provisional divorce is not from his wife but from Mendele. If it were not for their mutual poverty, Reb Leyb argues, he would never have entered into the contract in the first place, and so should be released from his obligation. Both their friendship pact and its eventual dissolution, then, are couched in the psychological and legal terms of traditional Jewish marriage and divorce.

This domestic farce involves a linguistic conflict as well. Mendele misreads Reb Leyb's abandonment, since Reb Leyb is leaving not to commit adultery with the mysterious woman whose company he is keeping but to become a Hebrew teacher—the woman turns out to be a Hebraist.

Most critics read "In the Days of the Noise" as testimony to Abramovitsh's antipathy toward the early Zionists in Odessa, particularly toward those among them who attempted to speak Hebrew among themselves. The linguistic move from Yiddish to Hebrew described in this
story, though, is figured as a quasi-sexual betrayal, a betrayal both of the
male bond and of proper Jewish masculinity. Reb Leyb's new Hebrew-
speaking world is far less sexually segregated than the old Yiddish-
speaking one, and what particularly disturbs Mendele is that the Hebrew
circle has broken with the sexual segregation of the traditional world.
While Mendele fails to meet the masculine standards of the Hebraists,
since he stammers in his attempts to speak Hebrew and lacks the physical
prowess to join a Zionist colony, he in turn sees Reb Leyb as something
less than a proper man. Mendele compares Reb Leyb's attempts to speak
Hebrew to a woman in the throes of childbirth, an act that also feminizes Mendele as participant: "I felt that Reb Leyb was a woman in labor who was having a difficult childbirth and I was the midwife, com-
passionately trying every which way to get the baby out."[25] The same
Mendele who in the Yiddish version of *The Travels* described the Hebrew
writers as more manly than himself, here, in this Hebrew story, mocks
the new Hebrew speaker as unnatural and womanish.

"In the Days of the Noise" not only reworks some of the motifs of
The Travels, it also echoes the triangulated scenario presented in "Notes
toward My Literary Biography." The drama of a single woman (the word
"matron" is used in both texts) who disrupts the bond between men
both mirrors and reverses the metaphorical conflict between Abramovitsh,
the lovers of Hebrew, and "Yehudit." In the biographical notes, however,
the woman is associated with Yiddish, whereas here she is associated
with Hebrew. (In both these scenarios, we might note, the woman may
embody language but herself remains voiceless, a medium of exchange
and bone of contention in a male world, a matrix for [pro]creating texts
but also the embattled arena of disputatious male ideologies.)

"In the Days of the Noise" ends with Mendele going back to the small
town of Kabtsiel where he belongs, as the Zionist assures him is proper,
while Reb Leyb stays in Odessa as a Hebrew teacher. The "divorce" pre-
figures the eventual mutual disentanglement of Hebrew and Yiddish, and
on similar grounds. When Reb Leyb argues that the connection between
himself and Mendele was born of historical compulsion, we might remember Achad Ha'am's similar argument that the connection between
the Jewish people and Yiddish had run its historical course.[26] But "In the

Days of the Noise" gives Mendele the last word, even if it was Reb Leyb who initiated the divorce. "There will always be a Kabtsiel," Mendele philosophizes, and thus always a place for himself and Yiddish. In this, Mendele denies the wisdom of the Hebraists, who saw Yiddish as the temporary language of the Jewish diaspora. Whatever one may think of the prophetic truth of Mendele's words, "In the Days of the Noise" provides a countercritique of Hebraism, though, significantly enough, in fictional form. If writing Yiddish renders Abramovitsh sexually suspect— of trafficking in the "woman's literature" and being seduced into an illegitimate tryst with the exotic, non-Jewish other—for Mendele, Hebrew is the perversion of natural speech and the Hebrew-speaking intelligentsia the realm of sexual license and the perversion of proper gender roles.

IV

During the last twenty years of his life, Abramovitsh set himself to recording or imagining his childhood experiences, writing a long and ultimately unfinished fictionalized autobiography, translating from Hebrew to Yiddish and vice versa as he progressed. The novel, called *In Those Days* in Hebrew and *Shlomo, Chaim's Son,* in Yiddish, has a complex publication history. It appeared in stages, with a Hebrew preface coming out in 1894, the same year as "In the Days of the Noise," and what would become the fourth and fifth chapters following five years later.[27] Considering Abramovitsh's involvement with the "language question" in the 1880s and 1890s, it is not surprising that the self-translated fictionalized autobiography that occupied his final years is both an exploration and product of the writer's bilingualism.

The preface starts familiarly enough, with Mendele alighting from a train in N——— (presumably Odessa), filled with the usual complaints and wry observations about travel and the big city. The effect of this opening is to reassure the audience that they are on familiar ground, even if the scene is a major metropolis. But Mendele's eventual destination could not be more unsettling: he proceeds to visit his writer-friend Reb Shloyme in his middle-class apartment, which is filled with philosophical and disputatious Hebrew writers.[28] It soon becomes clear that we are meant to read Reb Shloyme as none other than Sholem Yankev Abramovitsh. The effect of placing a deliberately transparent fictional representation of the author under the critical scrutiny of the first-person narrator who is presumably his creation is to plunge the reader into a hall of mirrors, confusing the categories of author and fictional character. The writer and Mendele discuss literature, not only abstractly but also in the most practical sense: Mendele agrees to help Reb Shloyme into print. The writer's consent to write his autobiography, if Mendele promises to do the work of publishing it, completes the reversal of figure and frame.

The meeting between Reb Shloyme and Mendele reunites a Europeanized Hebrew writer and his more traditional friend—and folk-hero narrator. The fact that the first-person narrator is a Yiddish speaker while the writer, described in the third person, is part of a Hebrew circle, suggests the complex asymmetry of Abramovitsh's bilingual authorship. By setting up an encounter between a Yiddish and a Hebrew writer, Abramovitsh could turn the tables on himself as invisible author and lay open the world of the Europeanized writer to his Yiddish narrator's ironic gaze. A pattern emerges: in the biographical notes, Abramovitsh defends his love for Yiddish against the harsh criticism of the "lovers of Hebrew"; in "In the Days of the Noise" his fictional Yiddish speaker takes potshots at an effeminate new Hebrew speaker. The preface takes this process a step further, satirizing a writer fortified in his comfortable circle of fellow authors and "lovers of Hebrew." This preface provides us with a "view from below" of the enlightened, serious, Hebrew-loving Odessa writers of which Abramovitsh was the very center.

The conversation among the Hebrew writers that forms an important part of the preface is interrupted by a yeshiva student looking for a place to sleep for the night, as itinerant yeshiva boys did in traditional Eastern Europe. The intrusion reminds Reb Shloyme of his own wanderings in his youth, which ultimately leads to his writing an autobiography. Like Mendele, the yeshiva boy is a double for the writer, entering, as Mendele had, without being immediately recognized by the older man. Abramovitsh, then, begins his fictionalized autobiography with a triply refracted authorial self, the fictional setting of a stormy Odessa night serving as a giant prism for reflecting a life split by abrupt transitions from one way of life, and one language, to another.

It may be significant that it is only with the entry of the young boy that the absence of women from the room becomes apparent; the writers become aware that a stranger has entered the house when they hear the voices of Reb Shloyme's wife and daughters, who are in the corridor, talking with the student. The men's belated perception of their absence provides a pretext for one of Mendele's philosophical digressions.

Immediately after the tea was finished, Reb Shloyme's wife and daughters felt themselves superfluous in the company of men who had matters of learning [*divrey torah*] to discuss and got up and left the room. There can be no doubt that wives of scholars have a portion in the world to come, for they certainly get nothing from their husbands in this one. Scholars [*talmiday chakhamim*] differ from uncultured people in a number of ways: the average man spends a lot of time talking with his wife, even more with the wives of others; but a scholar doesn't even talk to his own wife. . . . [I]f an ordinary person invites his friends over to play dice, his wife joins the quorum [*mitstarefet laminyan*] and plays with them all night long; the wife of a scholar, as soon as she serves the tea has no place there, and she hurries out of their sight. And that's how it was with Reb Shloyme's wife and daughters.[29]

The passage is obviously ironic, but the target is not immediately clear; it might be Reb Shloyme's imperfect relationship with his wife, but it could also be Mendele's reading of this relationship. And Mendele digs both at scholars who spend no time with their wives and at "the average person" who spends more time talking to other people's wives than to his own.

The most obvious level of irony, it seems to me, is generated by Mendele's "translation" of the modern setting into traditional Eastern European Jewish terms, addressing the writer as "Reb Shloyme" and describing this member of Odessa's middle-class Jewish intelligentsia in language more appropriate for a Torah scholar. Mendele may operate within a traditional conceptual structure, but to read him as a "simple Jew" underestimates the irony and self-consciousness of his posture. When Mendele declares that the wives of Torah scholars must receive a share in the world to come, we are prepared to hear that it is because of the merit of their diligent husbands, for Mendele's words sound like the opening of a pious rabbinic epigram. But Mendele comically frustrates our expectations by continuing with a wry critique of these scholars for not giving their wives anything "in this world."

Mendele's translation of modern Odessa customs into the conceptual framework of an earlier time stands in extreme contrast to Reb Shloyme's disconnection with the past. When Mendele first walks in, Reb Shloyme fails to recognize him. And Reb Shloyme has forgotten the old world to such an extent that when the yeshiva student asks to sleep in the school, the older man either cannot interpret the request or wishes to make clear the difference between a small-town yeshiva and a proper Talmud-Torah in the city: "Is my school some kind of hotel?"[30] he asks the boy sarcastically, although, as he later remembers, he himself had slept in synagogues and study houses in his youth.

Mendele's conflation of present and past reflects his quaint ignorance ("real" or feigned) of modern realities, but it also provides an insight into Reb Shloyme's unhappiness. Mendele's flattened perspective, ironic or not, allows him to see the continuity beneath the apparent disconnections of Reb Shloyme's modern *Weltanschauung*. Anyone can see that "Reb Shloyme" is no old-fashioned Torah scholar—he can barely even remember being a student—but his treatment of his wife and daughters suggests to Mendele that he might as well be one. That is, Mendele may be connecting the modern writer and the traditional scholar not because of his ignorance of modernity but because of his critical perspective on it. Mendele makes clear that the secular Hebrew literary world continues the traditions of religious Hebrew scholarship in at least one sense—by excluding women.

While the associations between Yiddish and Jewish women have often been noted, the connections between Hebrew and Jewish men have only rarely been subject to critical scrutiny. In this preface, however, Mendele describes the religious exclusion of women from the realm of the Holy Tongue as present in the arena of the secular Hebrew culture. The language of the masculine religious sphere, in Mendele's conflation, reappears in the still-masculine language of literary small talk (Mendele calls this "divrey-torah," the discourse surrounding Torah study).[31] The sexual segregation Mendele notes in Reb Shloyme's house adds another dimension to Abramovitsh's perceived sense that in writing Yiddish, he is betraying the world of important men, coming too close to those "ordinary" men who get enjoyment from female company. And Mendele's slightly risqué reference to extramarital flirtation ("the average man spends a lot of time talking with his wife, even more with the wives of others") reminds us of Abramovitsh's unsettling comparison of writing Yiddish with committing adultery.

Mendele's contribution to this version of the sexual drama of choosing a language sharply contrasts with his disapproval, in "In the Days of the Noise," of Hebrew as the realm of sexual license and disrupted gender roles. Here Mendele provides a critique, not of the stammering and feminized language of the new Hebrew speaker, but of the overly masculine language and social arrangement of the accomplished Hebrew writer who participates in the transmission of patriarchal Hebrew culture. What emerges in the two Hebrew fictional works Abramovitsh published in 1894 ("In the Days of the Noise" and the prologue to *In Those Days*) is a double-pronged attack, from two nearly contradictory positions, on the valorization of Hebrew among Abramovitsh's peers, the "lovers of Hebrew."

Abramovitsh wrote the prologue in Hebrew, the language he used to explain himself to his fellow writers. The autobiographical novel appeared first in Yiddish, although both the preface and the prologue were translated to provide a (never completed) text in both languages. The first sections of the fictionalized autobiography to appear, which would eventually become the fourth and fifth chapters of the novel, suggest that Abramovitsh envisioned this work as something of a *Bildungsroman*, detailing the educational influences of the young Shloyme in an Eastern European "portrait of the writer as a young boy." Chapters 4 and 5 of *In Those Days* present us with what we might call Shloyme's literary patrilineage and, more surprisingly, the somewhat obscured lines of his literary matrilineage. The fragmented image of the author presented in the prologue, with Mendele, Reb Shloyme, and the yeshiva student together setting the scene for Abramovitsh's autobiographical composition, gives way in these two chapters to a double world of literary influence, one explicitly marked by gender.

The first presents the young Shloyme's entry into the arena of masculine Jewish learning and describes his father's search for a teacher who will teach him biblical and not only talmudic texts; the chapter goes on to record the powerful impression an apocalyptic and visionary passage from Isaiah made on the young student, from which Shloyme formulates an image of God as "a powerful and terrible lord, full of rage and vengeance, holding his strap and letting loose a mighty blow for every sin."[32] Chapter 5 describes a different literary influence, this one transmitted to Shloyme not through official male channels but by his eavesdropping on the rituals of his mother and her circle of female friends. The two chapters, taken together, give an almost programmatic account of a young boy's introduction to the classic patterns of Ashkenazic bilingualism. Quoting extensively from both Hebrew and Yiddish religious texts, they are a map of the competing and complementary influences of the two literary traditions: the sublime biblical prose that shaped the Hebrew literary tradition and the intimate reworkings and translations of the Bible and liturgy for women that were such an important part of Yiddish literary tradition and a genre in which, we might recall, Abramovitsh himself participated.

The narrator is fully conscious of the effect his citation of Yiddish women's literature may have on his reader. At the end of the fifth chapter, the narrator uncharacteristically breaks the frame of the story to address the reader in a direct and passionate defense of Jewish women's traditions.

Now let him come and mock, whosoever might find it in his heart to say that the things mentioned here are nonsense. Let them bring forth such burning emotions, such pure and heartfelt emotions, hot tears, prayers, and love—love for Torah and wisdom, love for humanity, for the whole world of human beings! And all this belongs to whom? To Jewish women, daughters of Israel from the common people who, if you look at them from outside, seem to be nothing; if you look at them in the market, they seem quite ignorant. But if only we had many more of these women with such feelings and such words.
　Let those people, those people hear . . . and know what a Jewish heart means. Let them hear—and be silent![33]

Writers like Isaac Meir Dik directly addressed the female reader. In these chapters, the narrator is clearly speaking to an audience that views "simple women" with contempt. Rather than writing an autobiography whose "high" register matches the education of the audience the Europeanized author cultivated, however, *In Those Days* insists on the value of the "low" genres and uneducated readers of traditional Yiddish culture. Yet even this fierce defense of Yiddish women's religious literature (or orature) vacillates between serving as the spokesman for what lies hidden "inside the hearts" of Jewish women and looking at Jewish women "from the outside."

　The fifth chapter presents Yiddish women's history through its descriptions of the protagonist's mother, Sarah. Sarah is both an exemplary and a typical woman, who serves as a leader of women less familiar with the religious texts than she is and a pious transmitter of women's ritual practices. She is a woman learned in

all the *tkhines* of Erets-Israel, in the *Ma'ayan tahor*, in all the laws incumbent on a woman, she read the *Tsenerene*, the *Menoyras-hama'or* and all such books. She showed the women how to pray, what to say, when to get up, recited aloud for them and kept a lemon or some drops in the women's section for reviving herself or others if they felt faint.[34]

The narrator goes on to quote Sarah's candle-rolling prayer and to describe the female setting for the enactment of the ritual.

She cut many threads for each wick. Women, broken-hearted neighbors stood around her. She read aloud for them with a quivering voice deep from her heart:
　"Lord of the World, merciful God. May these candles which we are about to put in the synagogue in honor of your great Name and in honor of the

pure, holy souls arouse the holy fathers and mothers to pray for us from their graves so that no evil, trouble or suffering befall us and may our candle and our husbands' candle and our children's candle not be extinguished before their time, God forbid . . . [ellipses in the original]

"As I lay this thread to make a wick for our father Abraham, whom you saved from the fiery oven, so may you purify us from our sins and may our soul return to you as innocent as when it entered our body. By the merit of my laying this thread for our mother Sarah may God remember in our favor what she suffered when they led her dear son Yitzhak to the altar. May she intercede for us before You that our children not be kidnapped, not be taken from us, that they not be thrown far away from us like blind lambs."[35]

Ashkenazic women's personal prayers have often been read as unmediated expressions of feminine pain, yet Sarah's tkhine is both deeply traditional and subtly transgressive. It calls on the past (including the matriarchs, as is customary in these prayers, whereas traditional liturgy typically refers only to the patriarchs), but in the antinomian form of asking the dead ancestors to intercede for the living.[36] Moreover, the prayer audaciously sets the actions of God and of the woman performing the ritual on a level of symbolic equivalence, as if the woman were proposing an equal exchange of services: "As I lay this thread . . . so may you purify us." This passage is different in the later Hebrew version of the text, where the two parallel actions—his rescue of Abraham and his hoped-for salvation of the Jewish soul—both belong to God: "This wick I lay out for Abraham. Save us as you saved him." The Yiddish narration of Sarah's recitation of the text grants her more authority as well, describing her as singing "in her own tune" rather than, as in the Hebrew, "in a tune"—one not necessarily of her own composition. The Yiddish mother, then, is a creative, autonomous artist, acting, in a sense, on a par with God, while the Hebrew one more modestly follows the authority of an already established tradition.

The text itself, in both versions, leaves the question of the originality of this prayer ambiguous, perhaps deliberately so: is the fictional Sarah reading from a collection of women's personal prayers, perhaps the one mentioned in the catalog of books Sarah has mastered, or is she improvising her own prayer? In fact, the prayer Sarah recites appears to be taken in part from the seventeenth-century collection attributed to Sarah Bas-Tovim entitled *The Three Gates*, which appears on the list of books Sarah knows in the Hebrew version of this passage. The reference to Sarah as having had her son taken from her, though, is almost certainly not from the prayer collection, since it refers directly to the historical drafting of Jewish boys during the reign of Nicholas I (1825–

1855). By adding this reference, the prayer politicizes the spiritual heritage of its traditional texts in this passage. When Shloyme's mother invokes her namesake Sarah the Matriarch, whose son was also "kidnapped," to protect her own family from the army recruiters, she implicitly compares Abraham's pious willingness to sacrifice his son on God's orders with the opportunistic acts of Jewish flunkies carrying out the unfair and oppressive czarist edicts. The comparisons between God and the czar, and between Abraham and the *khapers,* are audacious and subversive in both languages. But in Abramovitsh's Hebrew version, the subversive quality is somewhat softened by adding, in the next phrase, Sarah's request for salvation on the basis of the meritorious piety of Isaac (described in various midrashim on Genesis), who stretched out his neck under Abraham's knife: "And for the sake of the bound [Isaac] on the altar who stretched out his neck under the knife have mercy on our children and make us worthy, Father, to hire a teacher for our sons to teach them Torah."[37] The Hebrew version thus places the Jewish woman's experience in a larger biblical and midrashic context, while the Yiddish views Sarah's loss of her son solely from her perspective. By focusing solely on Sarah's experience of her son's disappearance, the Yiddish version more directly and strongly supplies the female voice for a biblical narrative in which she never appears.

In fact, it would be wrong to read these differences as stemming either from the Yiddish writer's greater fidelity to an actual artifact of women's culture or from the Hebrew writer's conservative adherence to Jewish exegetical tradition. The Hebrew version of Sarah's prayer more closely resembles the Yom Kippur tkhine attributed to Sarah Bas-Tovim than the Yiddish version.[38] The Yiddish version, rather than being an unmediated primary artifact of female Ashkenazic religious expression, seems instead to be of Abramovitsh's composition, either from the memory of his mother's prayer or from a reworking of Bas-Tovim's prayer for the Yiddish audience of his day.

As tempting as it is to decide that Abramovitsh's Yiddish prayer captures a lost artifact of Jewish women's culture, the autobiography itself finally prompts a recognition that what is most Yiddish in it is also what is most stylized, most self-conscious, and most fictional. It is significant, after all, that what is pseudo, the pseudonym, the pseudoautobiographer, what is transparently fictional in the preface's gallery of characters, is connected with Yiddish while what is identified with the "real" belongs to the sphere of the Hebrew writer. For all the artificiality of Hebrew novelistic discourse in Abramovitsh's time, Yiddish still had a quality that lent itself to fictionalization, to romanticization, to a "folksiness" that is not so much authentic Eastern European Jewish culture, whatever that may be, as it is a construction of the authentic.

The features of Abramovitsh's moves from Hebrew to Yiddish and back again to a Hebrew made flexible by the intervening Yiddish writing are well known. The services that Yiddish, the "servant girl," performed for Hebrew, "the Lady," are the basic stuff of modern Hebrew literary historiography. But *In Those Days* reveals another part of the story, more rarely discussed, and that is Abramovitsh's second transition from Hebrew into Yiddish, of which this novel is the salient example. The Hebrew-Yiddish polysystem eventually ended in mutual disentanglement, with Hebrew asserting its autonomy from Yiddish and Yiddish from Hebrew. The Soviet Yiddish community, for instance, actively distanced their language from Hebrew, to the point of avoiding its Hebrew component and using Yiddish orthography for the Hebrew words they kept. But a similar distancing from Hebrew, though for different reasons, characterizes Abramovitsh's return to Yiddish. This return to Yiddish in the 1890s derived not from the utilitarian demands of the Eastern European Jewish Enlightenment but at least partly from an informed critique of the social arrangements and values associated with Hebrew. In both his Yiddish and Hebrew prose of the 1890s, Abramovitsh presents the Yiddish language and Yiddish literature as vying on equal terms with its Hebrew counterparts. And Abramovitsh's inclusion, or invention, of a feminine Yiddish counterpart to the more faithful Hebrew version of Sarah's tkhine and a feminine commentary on the canonical Hebrew tradition signifies his openness to these previously marginalized feminine traditions.

For the Eastern European Jewish community, Hebrew and Yiddish existed on a cultural and linguistic continuum; the demand for a national literature required that this continuum be split into two—and this affected Yiddish as much as Hebrew literature. What Abramovitsh the Hebrew writer of the biographical notes, "In the Days of the Noise," and the preface did for Abramovitsh the Yiddish writer of Sarah's remarkable prayer was to invest Yiddish writing with a self-consciousness that ultimately resulted in making it more Yiddish, as it were. Sarah Bas-Tovim's Yiddish prayer, which almost certainly provided the basis for Abramovitsh's Hebrew text, is actually a not atypical combination of Hebrew and Yiddish, with a large admixture of biblical and midrashic quotation. The Hebrew version translates the Yiddish sections into Hebrew, leaving the Hebrew quotations intact. The Yiddish, by contrast, removes most of these quotations, so that the resulting prayer contains everything in the original that was least traditional; without the extensive biblical allusions, the prayer is revealed as a conduit of a separate and distinctly feminine approach to the Jewish library. When the matriarch Sarah suffers the loss of her son, and the self-sacrificing piety of her son remains outside the text, the result renders the subversive aspects of Jewish women's prayer more visible. Thus what appears at first glance as the Jewish woman's freedom from an adherence to a canonical text and a resulting creativity of religious expression reappears, but this time in the person of the male Yiddish writer.

In this last work, Abramovitsh bids farewell to Mendele, but only to return more directly to the "women's literature" that is among Mendele's stock-in-trade. If, as Niger said, Abramovitsh brought the "altar and Holy Ark" into the "women's section" of Yiddish literature, it is also true that, by the end of his literary career, he had brought the zogerke, the women's prayer leader, back into Yiddish literature. More than that, Abramovitsh led the zogerke into the "men's section," the central and hegemonic space of Hebrew literature, where she had never been welcome before.

3 Baron "in the Closet"

An Epistemology of the "Women's Section"

The "women's section" [of the synagogue] was a kind of spiritual ghetto for women.

—Shmuel Niger, 1912

I

If Abramovitsh captured the hearts of his public by gaining—in his Mendele persona—a comfortable familiarity, Dvora Baron fascinated her readers by her singularity, by the very uniqueness of a woman's command of Hebrew in the heart of traditional Eastern Europe. To the image Frishman drew of Abramovitsh being borne aloft by thousands of admirers we can juxtapose the images of Baron's life: the young girl sitting alone in the women's section of the synagogue, listening to her father teach Torah; the fifteen-year-old who left her home to study secular subjects in the big city (with her parents' consent!); the young woman lying on a bed on a Friday night in Mariampol, surrounded by yeshiva boys eagerly displaying their modern Hebrew skills for their young and beautiful mentor; the frail recluse, shut in her apartment for decades as Tel Aviv grew and roiled around her. Whatever psychological idiosyncrasies shaped Baron's extraordinary life, it is hard to view this life as separate from the initial move she made, when barely into her adolescence, to become a Hebrew writer, the first woman to make a career for herself in Hebrew prose.

If Baron was exceptional, it was first of all by being born to an exceptional father, a small-town Lithuanian rabbi who had a radical and generous approach to his gifted daughter's education. A student of Baron's father describes how the young Dvora participated in the classes her father held in the town beit midrash.

Dvora would sit by herself, imprisoned in the "women's section," studying *Eyn ya'akov* [a collection of haggadic material in the Talmud] or midrash aloud. From time to time she would call over the partition: "Father" or "Benjamin!" [her brother] "What does this mean?" Frankly, I secretly envied her dedication, although I also couldn't help admiring her.[1]

The biographical notes assembled by Baron's daughter after the writer's death confirm this scenario, describing how Baron's father, "noticing her talents and nobility of mind, educated her as he would a boy; she studied the *Eyn ya'akov* and midrash with great diligence, and later the Talmud as well."[2] In her important biography of Baron, Nurit Govrin details the factors that enabled Baron to receive an education in traditional Hebrew and Aramaic texts.

The rare combination of understanding parents, a brother who was also a spiritual guide, and a girl who was also blessed with talents, eager for learning and iron-willed, was what made possible the very existence of a rabbi's daughter–Hebrew writer, whose knowledge of Hebrew and grounding in the religious sources were natural and primary. The solution to her acquiring the Jewish-Hebrew education normally given to a boy was to make a necessary compromise, which allowed her to receive an education without seriously overthrowing accepted social conventions.[3]

Baron's father had it both ways. He upheld the letter of the law by having her remain within the women's section in body ("imprisoned," as Moshe Gitlin puts it) while allowing her to break the tacit and, in some sources, explicit prohibitions against women's Torah study. The study hall was simultaneously open and closed to her, and the screen or partition that separated her from her brother and father served as a reminder of the marginal status dictated by her female body even as she transcended the partition in mind and voice.

Another biographical account adds an interesting dimension. According to a man who grew up in Baron's hometown of Ouzda, Baron's father was "a strange man" in yet another way: "All day he studied and taught Torah, but at night, after midnight, when the people of the town could see a light in their Rabbi's window, they knew that he was reading the novels of Shoymer, the folk writer, which were so beloved by women."[4] This unusual man not only allowed his daughter access to the normatively male arena of Torah study, he himself also crossed the line into the arena of Yiddish literature, apparently without hiding these excursions from his fellow townspeople.

Dvora Baron never gave direct fictional form to any of the experiences described in these biographical vignettes, though they are important for explaining, as Govrin puts it, "the very existence of a rabbi's daughter–Hebrew writer." However true these stories are, the account of Baron in the synagogue can serve as a metaphorical map for Baron's transgressions of the sexual and linguistic borders of Hebrew-Yiddish. The traversed partition can encode the ways in which Baron presents us, often simultaneously, with the exemplary and the exceptional, the normative and the transgressive moments of feminine experience. Baron lays bare the vigorously upheld yet continually negotiated boundaries of the sexually segregated social and textual order.

The women's section and the main area of a traditional Eastern European prayer or study hall represent no simple symmetrical division of the genders into "separate but equal" zones. Synagogue architecture sets off a male center, with the Holy Ark holding the Torah, the pulpit, and the other ritual accessories, from the female periphery, where the women serve as the audience for male religious practice. (The women's section in Eastern European synagogues was often a balcony or gallery.) A semipermeable barrier regulates the flow from male center to female periphery. In many cases, the Eastern European synagogue did double duty as synagogue and classroom or informal study hall. This arrangement came in handy for Baron. The design intended to organize communal prayer had the benefit, at least in her case, of providing space for qualified female participation in Torah study as well, although the use Baron's father made of this contingency was far from sanctioned or usual. The partition, during his classes, became more permeable than usual, since the young girl was allowed to call across the screen to her father and brother and thus participate, to a limited extent, in the give-and-take of traditional Torah study. Nevertheless, the barrier and all it represented remained in place.

My reading of Baron's work through the metaphor of the synagogue is not completely without precedent. Amalia Kahana-Carmon has used synagogue architecture to describe modern Hebrew fiction, although of a later date. Kahana-Carmon argues that the hierarchies underlying synagogue architecture continue to govern collective Jewish practices, even at their most secular. Modern Hebrew literature, following the model of the synagogue, ordains that writing, like prayer, must speak of and for the collective, which is firmly associated with its male leadership. Kahana-Carmon explains that, in such an environment, women's speech and women's experience are necessarily seen as peripheral.

The supplications of the individual are preordained as trivial or inferior, compared to the central act, collective prayer. And this central activity—where does it take place? In the synagogue, a forum out of bounds for women.

Being a woman, her one place in this arena is in the women's gallery. As a passive observer, she does not contribute anything. Someone else, acting in the name of all Israel, speaks also on her behalf.[5]

In insisting on the continuities between traditional and "modern" Jewish thought structures, Kahana-Carmon illuminates the patriarchal ideologies underlying the Hebrew canon. The reception of Baron's Hebrew work was certainly influenced by its deviation from the masculine norms of her literary generation. The collective biography of the Hebrew writer in Eastern Europe describes the young writer's encounter with the Talmud, and, on the sly, with Haskalah literature, typically in the yeshiva in which he received the Orthodox education that would provide him with the building blocks he would later use in writing Hebrew.[6] This familiar narrative pinpoints the break with religious tradition, which usually occurred in adolescence, as the formative conflict from which modern secular Hebrew literature arose. Alan Mintz describes what he calls the "apostasy narrative" of the young men who were to become secular Hebrew writers.

Typically they originated from the most devout and scholarly circles of Jewish society, and many distinguished themselves as child prodigies of talmudic learning in whom the pride and resources of family and community were heavily invested. Often already in adolescence the "infection" of religious doubt was contracted through contact with Haskalah writings; the process was hastened after the writers left their towns and villages for the yeshiva and there formed bonds with other youths who harbored the same hesitations.[7]

This painful but creative rupture with the past often revealed itself in the intertextual strategies by which secular Hebrew writers reworked the religious canon of Hebrew and Aramaic sources. Modern Hebrew literary texts commonly position themselves as both inside and outside the chain of Hebrew literary history, rereading the Bible or postbiblical texts through a swerve empowered by the process of secularization.

Baron also left her home and religious background in midadolescence, and undoubtedly had male friends whose lives followed the pattern Mintz lays out. Her work, however, immediately strikes the reader as different from that of her male counterparts. Whereas many of the major fiction writers of her time (Y. Ch. Brenner, Sh. Y. Agnon, U. N. Gnessin, etc.) are more or less explicitly concerned with the aftermath of their male protagonists' break with religion, Baron tells stories about the traditional religious world. For a literary audience accustomed and eager to recognize the collective apostasy narrative in a literary text, Baron's work might well have seemed timid, outdated, and populated with the ignorant small-town folk the new generation of Hebrew readers longed to leave behind.

Baron's work, though, is neither conservative nor nostalgic. In story after story, she deals with an earlier and arguably more radical break than the one her readers were conditioned to recognize. A creative swerve, generated by her position of insider/outsider to the Hebrew literary tradition, did guide her writing. In Baron's case, the swerve was a function not only of secularization but also of a gendered exteriority to this tradition. Her stories read and counterread tradition not by nostalgically or bitterly describing, as her male counterparts did, a backward but coherent and unified traditional universe. Baron's "break with tradition" is already inherent in her experience of this tradition, either because she could not fail to notice its asymmetrical gender order or because of her own antinomian encounter with it.

Revisionist readings of religious texts already pervaded even the most "traditional" of female relations to the canon, as I argued earlier. Women's devotional prayers, for instance, forged a new approach to God based on intimacy and direct address. In drawing on this religious women's culture, Baron could participate in the modernist project of rereading Jewish tradition from within an apparently traditionalist discourse. And since the secular Hebrew circles Baron encountered in Lithuania were almost as male dominated as Torah study circles, it is not surprising that her creative and ironic misreadings should be directed toward the Hebrew writings of her male predecessors and contemporaries. Baron's subtle subversions of Hebrew literary texts through seemingly naive and pious characters (many of them female) do as much to unsettle Hebrew literary tradition, I argue, than the most overtly modernist Hebrew literature of her time.

To read Baron as simply a misunderstood and misread modernist is to ignore the degree to which she allowed for, even colluded in, critical "misreadings" of her work. By failing to set her stories in the contemporary Zionist community, Baron actively resisted the most overt of the ideological demands of Hebrew modernism for years after she migrated to Erets-Israel in 1911. As the literary editor of the Socialist-Zionist journal, the *Young Worker*, Baron was well aware of these demands. Govrin records the tepid public response to the first story Baron published in Palestine, entitled, appropriately enough, "In Which World?" One letter to the editor registered a reader's disappointment with the content of the first issue of *Moledet* (Homeland), a journal for youth, apparently with Baron's story in mind:

We thought that a journal for young people published in Palestine, which carries the title *Moledet* and is directed to the new young generation of the land and its spiritual renewal, would itself excel in providing a fresh new perspective, and would present us in its first issue with a refreshing story or essay about our new lives. And the first story the editor gives us is once again about the Diaspora, from that old painful sorrowful Diaspora life! God in heaven, when will there be an end to these stories? We're sick to death of them![8]

If the modernist Hebrew poet David Fogel was marginalized during his own lifetime because he remained in the diaspora, territorially removed from the Palestinian center and even the main Eastern European and American peripheries, Dvora Baron was marginalized because she continued to write about the diaspora from the very heart of Tel Aviv. Baron came to Palestine earlier than many of the Hebrew writers who are associated with the Palestinian literary center; moreover, she wrote the largest share of her work and published all her collections in Palestine. Yet Gershon Shaked includes his analysis of her work in the volume of his historiographical study devoted to diaspora writers rather than situating her in the Erets-Israeli volume of the series. Shaked's final appraisal of her work might shed some light on this apparent miscategorization: "It is possible that Baron is one of those writers who walk at the edge of the road, who leave no heirs or followers, although their clear footprints are readily seen on the grounds of our literature."[9] Baron, for all her geographic centrality to the Hebrew literary scene of her time, left a clear impression of and on "the edge of the road." Shaked's situating of her work in the diaspora may well be a response to his perception of her writings as themselves "in exile."

Baron's marginal stance as a woman writer, as a bilingual writer in a militantly monolingual environment, as a chronicler of the diaspora at the heart of Zionist activism, as a modernist whose experimentation took directions that were not always immediately identifiable cannot be entirely explained by the prejudices of her literary environment. Baron's modernist techniques and protofeminist political content were overlooked not only because these techniques were different from those of her literary generation or because they were unexpected in the writings of a woman but also because she cloaked herself in—or ironically reappropriated—traditional, "feminine" and subcanonical forms, genres, and styles. The trade-off for risking having her works misread is that Baron called attention (for those who were paying attention) to the subversive potential of the denigrated models she chose as her own. The model of the performative site of the synagogue may once again be aptly called into service here. Baron alternated between transgressing the borders of the gendered (and generic) spaces assigned to women and retreating, often ironically, to the generic and stylistic "women's section."

II

Baron began to publish Hebrew short stories in 1902, when she was just fifteen, and Yiddish stories in 1904. The peculiarities of Baron's status of a "rabbi's daughter–Hebrew writer" are evident from her very earliest Hebrew work. In 1903, "Three Sisters" appeared, a story that established Baron's credentials in at least three areas: as a Jewish girl versed in traditional Hebrew and Aramaic texts, as a worldly reader of modern European literature, and as an acute observer, especially of the female sphere. "Three Sisters" bears the epigraph " 'Women are envious beings' (*Midrash raba, Lekh lekha* 45:5, 10)," as if the young female author were immediately presenting her scholarly calling card to the Hebrew reading public.[10] The story also draws on Chekhov's work of the same title, which appeared in 1901, and demonstrates the author's ambitious efforts to emulate the Chekhovian style in favor with Hebrew writers of the time. Further, although Baron's characters are all female, they experience a range of disappointments and frustrations that might seem beyond the range of a teenage girl: spinsterhood, an unhappy marriage, sexual envy.

Readers who knew nothing about Baron were often shocked to discover how young she was. Baron's editor Y. Bershadsky, who had never met the writer personally, insisted in 1905 that a young girl could not have written the story Baron had sent him, entitled "A Quarreling Couple"; and if she had, her writing was evidence that "without a doubt she had already known a man."[11] While Bershadsky was merely expressing the common assumption that writers must have experienced some form of what they describe, his sexual speculations can give us some idea of what a young girl entering the early twentieth-century world of Hebrew letters might expect to encounter. "Three Sisters," in demonstrating Baron's possession of a variety of intellectual and experiential tools, also pinpointed her as a woman who had failed to remain "in her place."

Many of Baron's stories work as quasi-illustrations of biblical or postbiblical verses or proverbs, but "Three Sisters" is the earliest and arguably most salient example of this intertextual practice. At first reading, the story appears to treat the epigraph about women being envious creatures as a prooftext for which the writer, in formulaic homiletic style, furnishes three simple illustrative examples. The number three, typical of folkloric convention, is presumably enough to qualify as evidence bolstering the claim. Thus the writer uses her privileged insider view of women to support the midrashic text and the wisdom of the rabbis who produced it, a perhaps unexpected benefit of female Torah study. By the same token, in her application for membership to the circle of midrashic expanders of the Hebrew canon, Baron is in turn supported by her text, since the relative obscurity of the quotation can serve to demonstrate the breadth of her learning.

At the same time, the epigraph attests to the difficulty inherent in the phenomenon of the female "yeshiva student." The narrative and prooftext meet, after all, at the most uncomfortable juncture imaginable between a female writer and a masculine tradition. On one hand, the narrative highlights the gender of its author by granting us access to a female world; on the other, the epigraph, in utter deadpan, presents midrashic discourse at its most omnisciently misogynist.

Baron, or the imago of the rabbi's daughter/writer, appears most forcefully neither in the epigraph nor in the story proper but rather in the multiple gaps between rabbinical citation, Chekhovian narrative, and female signature. At the very outset, no reader can help noticing the space between the story's literary language—Hebrew—and the author's female signature beneath it. And in what amounts to very much the same thing, the story generates tension between a talmudic epigraph placing women as the transparent objects of male critical inquiry and a female-authored account of three women that proceeds to both confirm and undermine the rabbis' grand pronouncement on the subject of the feminine character.

"Three Sisters" is not just a "Jewish" text, however. The story places the young author in the ranks of the new generation of Hebrew writers who were reading the shtetl, not according to Abramovitsh, but with Chekhov's ear for the world-weary and inconsequential chatter of the restless and hopeless young. "Three Sisters" echoes the Chekhov play in title, structure, and tone. The opening lines of Baron's story are closer to spare stage directions than to the descriptive catalogs of Abramovitsh's work and of Baron's own later stories: "In a small room, Miss Goldberg sits and reviews her lesson. Across from her sits Levin, her friend." Chekhov's play begins, we might recall, with Olga correcting her students' papers while Masha and Irena sit lost in thought. Baron's narrative is rendered almost entirely through the sort of dialogue, punc-

tuated by ellipses and always on the verge of trailing off altogether, that
is Chekhov's signature.

Levin, who had been sitting quietly until now, began to drum her fingertips
on the table and spoke.
"Forget the lesson, Goldberg; let's just talk."
"And how about the lesson?"
"Don't worry, you'll know the lesson, I'll be responsible . . . "
"Anything new?"
"There's almost nothing new."

For all its self-conscious Chekhovian influence, however, it would be
wrong to see this story as simply another text about the disruptive effect of modernity on the sensibilities of a traditionally educated young
writer. A male Hebrew writer who moves from *Midrash raba* to a description of a group of young former yeshiva students mired in Chekhovian ennui might be making that point. Baron's juxtaposition of the
two literary influences cannot be explained solely through the apostasy
model. What is unusual about Baron's genesis as a Hebrew writer is that
her immersion in religious texts was itself a "modernity effect," reflecting her father's qualified version of an Enlightenment tolerance. For
Baron to quote the midrash already presents a challenge to its authority,
however mildly and deferentially she utilizes the text.

What is most subversive about Baron's text is not any explicit feminine protest she expresses against rabbinic pomposity, it is her unique
epistemological stance, her multiple avenues of knowledge. She knows
the text of *Midrash raba,* just as she demonstrates her familiarity with
Chekhov, and she has access to the female experience both texts claim
to describe. Baron's story does not deny that "women are envious": the
three women described exhibit definite propensities for envy. What most
differentiates the narrative from its epigraph is its evaluative stance:
where the midrash is absolutist and judgmental, Baron is psychological
and reserves explicit moral judgment, using Chekhov's dry delivery to
distance the narrator from both the characters and the prooftext.

Baron's story follows the three unmarried Goldberg sisters in the
course of a day in which they meet various female acquaintances, each
of whom is better off than they are in some way. Although each sister
is indeed envious in her own way, they never express their jealousy, leaving the narrator to identify their sighs, tears, and glances as signs of
suppressed envy. By the end of the story, their poverty and spinsterhood, combined with the blind insensitivity of their luckier acquain-

tances, win the reader's sympathy for the envy they understandably feel. In the course of apparently bolstering the masculine authority of the quoted text by drawing the curtains open on the female experiences it claims to understand, Baron undermines the superior tone of the midrash and reverses its emotional charge. The condemnation implicit in the midrash is redirected against a social order that unequally distributes material wealth, punishes women for failing to marry and oppresses them if they do (in the last example, the unmarried eldest sister and her married friend each envy the other's state), and finally, sees fit to criticize women for their human reactions to an unfair social and economic system. Envy is a possible, even a likely, result, in other words, of social, economic, and sexual marginality. Put in this way, the rabbinic diagnosis of women is less illuminating of "female nature" than of women's place in a social order the rabbis themselves are complicitous in maintaining.

Baron's first collection of Hebrew stories appeared in 1927, twenty-five years after she first began publishing short stories. The opening story of *Stories* is entitled "In the Beginning," signaling the writer's extravagant claim for her own literary work as a quasi-divine act.[12] The story echoes the two creation stories in Genesis: the first describes God creating the first human as a "male and female" (Gen. 1:27); the second establishes the hierarchy between Adam and his female partner, born of Adam's rib (Gen. 2:22). "In the Beginning" begins not with an egalitarian narrative, however, but with a female-centered one, describing a new bride's arrival in a poverty-stricken shtetl where her young husband has just received a post as rabbi. The story begins with the woman's unhappy perspective.

> Is it any wonder that the Rebetsin [rabbi's wife] of little Zhuzhikovka, when she saw the ruin of a *kehilah* [community] house and its neglected courtyard, should have stood tall and stubborn by the door and refused to enter.
>   But she did go in later. She took off her hat, revealing a blond wig with soft curls—and went in. But afterwards, when the welcoming party ended and everyone went home—she dropped in her city clothes to the naked bench in the community room and cried and cried, without cessation and without easing off, while he, her young husband, stood beside her in his silk caftan, girded in the sash of a rabbi—and at a loss for ideas.[13]

This description stops here and abruptly begins again, as it were, from the beginning; this time, the narrator includes a mildly ironic self-exhortation.

This story should begin in a different version, a more fitting one—as follows:
     When the new rabbi was supposed to arrive in town to take up his rabbini-
cal duties, the head of the community ordered that all the streets and the
synagogue be swept as if it were the eve of Passover.[14]

The first version, which focuses on the rabbi's wife's experience, changes
the typical center/margin relationship that organizes many of the narratives about a young man or couple moving back to the provinces. Here
it is the wife who is the educated and cultured big-city person forced to
confront the narrow confines of shtetl life, a role more usually assigned
to the young maskil. Her husband's official status is mentioned only to
be immediately contrasted with his helplessness before his weeping wife.
     The narrative that "begins again," however, places the male and his
exalted occupation as the central figure of a more distanced and conventionally told story. This second version provides a panoramic view of the
shtetl, omnisciently relating the sequence of events—unlike the first version, which mentions the welcoming party only to set the stage for the
Rebetsin's tears. These two openings thus present a doubled perspective
on the same events: one female and subjective, the other vacillating between a male and an omniscient or communal perspective. They are also
stylistically distinguished from each other. The first version is presented
in a folksy, conversational style behind which the Yiddish is clearly audi-
ble. The story begins with this passage:

About my mother, the Rebetsin of Zhuzhikovka, they say in my little
hometown this:
     She, the Rebetsin, was brought here some years ago from some faraway
large city in the country of Poland.[15]

The generic affiliations of this passage, with its implied collective narrator, unspecified time, and vagueness about details that are not readily
available ("from some city"), are with the folktale. But while this subcanonical affiliation links Baron with orature, which is often affiliated
with women, it also frees her from the conventions of premodernist realism, allowing her to experiment in the flexible syntax associated with
the conversational mode and substitute unexpected gaps and juxtaposi-
tions for the catalogs of realia of the *nusach* style, the normative Hebrew
prose idiom forged by Abramovitsh and his immediate followers. How,
then, do we read Baron's move toward a more conventional perspective
and mode of narration after four paragraphs? On one hand, her "self-

correction" highlights the stylistic and perspectival transgressions of the first "beginning," placing the entire narrative squarely in the camp of self-conscious modernist experimentation. On the other hand, the narrator, once having chosen a "more fitting version," continues her story with it, making us wonder to what extent we are supposed to approve of "propriety" in storytelling. In any case, it is telling that the first version of the story aligns a woman's perspective with a simulation of Yiddish syntax and modernist experimentation while in the second version the masculine perspective and normative premodern Hebrew syntax dominate.

In "The First Day," a story that appeared in the same collection as "In the Beginning," Baron again juxtaposes modernist and antimodernist elements, although in different ways. If "In the Beginning" shifts generic affiliations from the folktale to the socially conscious realist narrative, "The First Day" represents Baron's ironic relation to two subcanonical genres: children's literature and the memoir. Baron, whose marginalization derived in part from her use of children as narrators (she also often wrote for children), here took her own practice to its limit by having her story narrated by a day-old baby.[16] If her practice of writing from the perspective of young shtetl girls contributed to the perception that her work was thinly veiled autobiography or naive children's literature, then "The First Day" subjects this perception to a reductio ad absurdum. Baron's first-person chronicle of a day-old baby girl cannot be ascribed to memory; nor could the experiences related here have come from family stories—in one passage, the narrator describes the discomfort of her too-tight swaddling clothes. Among the effects of such scenes in "The First Day" is to expose the fictionality of memoiristic conventions.

Feminist readings of Baron that privilege her explicit protest narratives are no less immune to misreading than the male critics who see her focus on domestic life and her apparent adherence to conventional forms as reflecting a modesty appropriate to a woman writer. What interests Baron is precisely the tenuousness of traditional textual and social structures—both in the area of distinct masculine and feminine spheres and in the separation between the modern and traditional, modernist and antimodernist realms. Thus "The First Day," despite its explicit feminist protest against the lesser valuation of daughters than sons, presents a complex universe in which masculine and feminine discourse cannot be easily separated. The last few paragraphs of the story describe the baby's father, whose voice floats over the partition to his new daughter, singing a song that is not about "sons or daughters."

For a long time my father continued to walk back and forth on the other side of the partition, singing to himself an ordinary, unimportant tune, like one that might be sung to calm someone or put them to sleep, and which comes easily and fluently to every father's lips. His other tune, the extraordinary one, the one which in the course of years, during those nights in my bed, would drench my sadness like wine, came afterward, a few hours later, as he sat by the light of the lamp at the table over his books, no longer pondering the fate of sons or daughters on this earth but rather that of humanity in general.

Reproachful, piercing, laced with gentleness—as if with a magical wand he lifted the veil from my future for an instant, and I peeked:

Gloom and greyness, with no passage or exit . . . —and I was shaken.

At the sound of my cries Father came from the other side of the partition and rocked me, going back, in an instant, to the tune from before, the ordinary one, the one every father knows by heart.

—There, there, it's nothing, it's nothing, he soothed me, soothed me and sang, until I calmed down, and exhausted—fell asleep. So ended the first day of my life.[17]

The partition in this small house is a graphic image of the poor family's makeshift quarters. However tempting it might be to read the partition also as the already-erected barrier of gender between the listening daughter and the father who is lost in his books, the father's words themselves militate against such a reading. But his ability to transcend the strictures of gender, if only in solitude and meditation, is not necessarily utopian: it is the tune that comes to his lips in this mood, "no longer pondering the fate of sons or daughters on this earth but rather that of humanity in general," that terrifies his daughter.

For all of the apparent solidity of Baron's described shtetl universe, the narratives generally take their shape in the liminal spaces where old forms break down or where the conflicting demands of men and women, tradition and modernity, the urbane and the provincial confront each other. "Feminist" or "misogynist" discourses in Baron cannot be simply identified with male and female characters; instead, texts supportive of or antagonistic to male or female interests form a broad and ramified palette from which male and female speakers may draw. That this should be so does not neutralize the political potency of the texts, nor does it essentially alter the social hierarchy. Baron, far from being the recorder of a static or even stagnant society, presents us with a system in flux, and male/female relations are often the points of stress or the incentives and markers of change. In "The First Day," the grandmother quotes from the rabbis, "may their memory be blessed," to her exhausted and intimidated daughter-in-law.

Having spent her life in the vicinity of learned men, and thus listening to their conversations, my grandmother also knew some sayings from the discourse of our sages, may their memories be blessed, in the matter of a daughter and her value in life.

Thus, for example, she knew, that if the son is compared to wine, then the daughter is nothing but vinegar; if a son is as wheat, then the daughter—is like unto barley.

True: there is a need for wine and a need for vinegar, but the need for wine is greater than for vinegar; so too, one needs both wheat and barley but—the need for wheat is greater than that for barley.

Alas, the erudition of this old rabbi's wife was awesome. Like giant boulders rolled the sayings from her mouth, one heavier and more frightening than the next.[18]

Lost in translation is Baron's juxtaposition not only of two women's responses to the birth of a daughter but also of two different Hebrew styles. The grandmother's words are composed of ponderous quotations from religious texts. Like the writers of an earlier generation, the grandmother speaks in *shibuts* form, building sentences both by direct quotation and by adapting formulaic talmudic connectives to make her point. A reader familiar with this tradition would not only recognize the quotations in substance and form but also hear the singsong intonation by which the grandmother's logic would impress itself on her listener. The grandmother's speech, in short, is thoroughly imbued with the weighty style of masculine Torah discourse, just as her words are drawn from the most misogynist of its texts. Her relationship with this discourse is an uneasy blend of appropriation and internalization, as if she herself could escape the rabbinic judgments only by the boldest affiliation with their authority.

The daughter-in-law, by contrast, is represented only implicitly in the "combined perspective" (linking the daughter-narrator and the new mother) of the sentences that follow. The style of these sentences moves toward the modernist flexibility Baron's generation introduced into the Hebrew idiom, a flexibility that is largely derived from Yiddish: her second sentence is structured according to the Yiddish rules for word order. The ambiguity of the younger woman's response—*nora* means both terrible and awesome—and the hyperbole of the narrator's tone have something of the irony that often characterizes Yiddish, especially in relation to Hebrew.[19] By describing the rabbinical words as awesome/terrible, the less-educated mother can both acknowledge and ironically undermine their textual and sexual authority. As in "In the Beginning," Baron alternates between two Hebrew idioms, one associated with a masculine world of textual allusion and the premodern prose style of early generations of Hebrew writers and another informed by Yiddish conversational style, a feminine, somewhat ironic discourse that challenges and responds to the first style.

In the next paragraph, the desolate mother is comforted to remember that at the birth of her first daughter, her husband had explained to her that "what was meant by 'And God blessed Abraham with everything [*bakol*],' was that He gave him a daughter named 'Bakol.' " The father, in this passage, refers to the commentary on Genesis 24:1 that reads the word *bakol* as referring to a daughter by that name. But the commentators are divided on how to interpret the passage, with the medieval commentator Rashi citing a different midrash that equates the word *bakol* numerically with the word for son. Thus the father chooses only the midrash that will support his own desire to celebrate the birth of a daughter, a choice that also lends support to his wife. If this passage represents a masculine manipulation of the patriarchal Jewish tradition, it also signifies the uses to which a well-versed woman author can put the Hebraic intertextual universe. Similarly, the paternal voice's triumph over the grandmother's misogyny can indicate that, as a man, his message takes precedence over a woman's, or that his feminism saves the day. In either case, the father's kindness to his wife counters the grandmother's misogyny, making it difficult to map out a symmetrical equation between gender and gender ideologies.

In "Family," the phenomenon of feminine ventriloquism of masculine discourse takes the form of a female character who acts as guardian of community values.[20] Batya, who chastises Dinah for failing to procreate, is presented as a student of her itinerant-preacher father: "She learned to orate from him and at family gatherings she loved to hold forth while the others were compelled to listen compliantly." After Dinah has remained childless for five years, Batya comes to visit "armed, as the importance of the occasion dictated, with the ancient umbrella she had inherited from her father, and which, in her hands, acquired the form of a chastising rod."[21] To complete the image of the phallic woman, competing on equal terms with male discourse because she is willing to adopt it unquestioningly, Batya adds her own voice to the Torah reading in synagogue, telling a parable about a tree that fails to bear fruit and is thus struck down, "waving her palm rapidly until Dinah, who was standing near her, flinched, as if Batya were ready with the axe against her."[22] Batya's adoption of a murderous male discourse finally forces Dinah to abandon the women's section, so that female companionship or sym-

pathy is denied her as well. Thus women's participation in patriarchal traditions is viewed ambivalently as a possible threat to female soli-
darity and as consolidating and universalizing male control over female
lives.

What might be seen as the biological misfortune of Dinah's childlessness is revealed, in Batya's words, as a transgression against a textually
inscribed order. It is significant, then, that when her salvation finally
comes, it is through a malfunction in this textual system. When after
ten years of childlessness her husband is compelled—against both of
their wishes—to divorce Dinah, the divorce is annulled when the bill of
divorcement is shown to contain an inadvertently misshaped letter. The
narrator writes, "Sometimes drowning people suddenly see a hand or a
board floating on the water, or people engulfed in fire see a window or
hole in the wall; here it happened in the form of a letter that was inserted
in the wrong place and stuck out of the straight line."[23] The last phrase
"yats'ah min hashurah" (it [or she, since "letter" in Hebrew is feminine]
went out of the line), dramatizes the confluence of social and textual
transgressions. Earlier in the story, Dinah is herself described as being
outside the line of dancers that includes her husband at a wedding party:
"Now she was outside the line, a link that had slipped from its place."[24]
The possibility of slipping out of one's place, which is devastating for
her in the social and biological realm, is what saves her in the textual
realm. The "failures" that occur in the biological order have their share
in the textual order; as it turns out, this is a fortunate slip of the pen.
The connection between the body and the text is dramatized in this description of the flawed bill of divorcement.

The old scribe did not immediately understand what had happened and tried
to set the dangling line stroke back in its place, and then my father put out
his hand and raised the parchment and the assembled crowd, in their fear
and trembling, saw that one end of a letter had been cut off like the leg of a
living being that had been dislocated, and it was bleeding ink [*shotetet dyo*]
and darkening like a wound in the middle of the text.[25]

The story makes brilliant use of the Jewish tradition of finding
equivalences between the body and the text. The dislocated leg aptly
stands in for the couple whose connection to each other the manuscript
is supposed to dissolve. But the story also explores the discontinuities
between body and text. While the manuscript is "bleeding ink," the narrator describes the husband's face as drained, "with no drop of blood in
it."[26] The Talmudists and Kabbalists were concerned with demonstrating

the equivalences of the Torah with the perfect (male or divine) body. Baron, by contrast, is more interested in recognizing the place of imperfection, dismemberment, sterility, transgression, and the feminine in this textual-physical realm. Human experience, the story seems to imply, does not always match the texts that attempt to govern it; and when correspondences are found, the match may be in the very flaws of each system.

Baron's story establishes correspondences not only between bodies and texts but also among texts themselves, responding to earlier treatments of the issue of patriarchal control over marriage. "Family" alludes to Y. L. Gordon's well-known mock-epic poem of 1868, "The Tip of the Yod." Gordon's "passionate threnody on the plight of the Jewish woman"[27] begins with the famous question "Jewish (or Hebrew) woman, who knows your life?" and relates the tragic separation of two lovers when the woman's divorce from her first husband is declared invalid. The now-missing husband, Hillel, had signed his name with the "defective" rather than the "plene" spelling, and so the yod, the smallest (and most insignificant, Gordon implies) letter, is missing. Gordon's poem, a Jewish version of the kingdom lost for want of a nail, is a melodramatic attack on the hairsplitting orthodoxy of his time.

Baron's story, at first reading, appears to reverse Gordon's attack, since the hero of the story is the rabbi who, by discovering the mutilated letter, allows the couple to remain together. Rabbis, this rabbi's daughter might be saying, can as easily decide in favor of human needs as against them. "Family" lends itself to a different intertextual reading, however. In Baron's story the textual flaw is what enables the loving couple to remain married despite the practice of divorce prescribed for childless couples. By contrast, in Gordon's poem, the flawed text keeps his couple apart. The disputed divorce provides Gordon with the opportunity to demonstrate the wrong-headed legalism of the rabbinic world.

The presiding judge, a Kabbalist, who was versed in the "secret wisdom"
  Decided according to the AR"I that Hillel was spelled without a yod,
And the second judge agreed according to *Bedek habayit*—
  And the two of them decided that the divorce was kosher;
Only Rabbi Vafsi decided that Hillel was spelled with a yod
  As the ZA"M and the SA"M had decreed, in accordance with the
  Shulchan Arukh.
And he raged at them and said that he was amazed
  That both of them could have forgotten the decision of the *Arukh.*
And so he stood his ground like a porcupine and like a planted tree
  And shouted out loud in Yiddish, "The divorce is invalid!"[28]

For Gordon, then, the problem of Jewish textual authority over sexuality and gender roles is one that pits lenient interpretations against strict ones. The implication is that if only the lenient approach were adopted, the loving couple could be reunited. Men, in Gordon's narrative, retain control over determining what constitutes a textual (and sexual?) lack. For Baron, masculine textual authority over women's lives is itself the problem, one that no paternalistic manipulation of Hebrew or Aramaic texts can resolve. The only way in which women's concerns can be reflected in this male universe is when the text is disrupted. It is when the scribe's hand fails to perform its prescribed role according to "the letter of the law" that the divorce papers finally reveal something of the painful story occluded in the document's perfect state. Only the slip of the pen can signify the painful separation of Dinah (who has no part in the "official" document) and her uneducated husband, inadvertently pointing to this experience as the bloody mutilation of a living organism.

In "Family," as in "Three Sisters," the gaps between masculine and feminine knowledge are implicit in the narrative but are never directly described. In "Agunah" (Abandoned Woman), Baron places the epistemological gap at the heart of the story and translates architectural divisions into hermeneutic differences.[29] The narrative begins with a description of the bitter late autumn in the village and the muddy road along which a traveling preacher makes his way to the prayer hall, and takes the reader through the prayers and the opening remarks of the preacher. After setting up the scene from a distanced, universalizing, and omniscient perspective, the narrator moves to the women's section of the synagogue, where Dinah, the rabbinical judge's elderly wife, sits alone, literally and figuratively "in the dark," since she does not understand the prayers she can nevertheless recite by heart. The narrator describes Dinah in her peripheral, alienated, and disempowered relation to the religious narrative unfolding within the synagogue. The physical barrier separating men and women in the prayer hall, then, is also an epistemological one, denying women access to textual intercourse. To the extent that communication does exist, the multiple barriers dividing the sexes produce refractions and "warped" readings, like the light that comes into the women's section obliquely and already diluted. Dinah can hear the prayers and the preacher's sermon, but their meaning is closed to her.

Her two eyes look directly at the mouth of the dear Jew, standing at the pulpit beneath. The biblical verses and rabbinical sayings are closed to her, though, and rest uneasily in her mind, like the slices of stale bread in her husband's house—in her toothless mouth. But no matter: she has her sock and ball of thread with her, and here she is in the meantime, knitting.[30]

Not only is the bread dry, her mouth is toothless the narrative tells us, signaling deficiencies in both the Torah and her desire or ability to partake of it. And even the bread, like the Torah, comes from her husband's house: she is an unequal participant in both the domestic and the religious spheres. The phrase, in fact, is a homely concretization of any of the numerous aphorisms linking bread and Torah, either as equally necessary and good forms of sustenance or as representing materiality and spirituality, respectively ("Where there is no bread, there is no Torah," "Not hunger for bread . . . but for the word of God," etc.).[31] The Torah as stale bread metaphor is familiar in principle, but the negative valence of both tenor and vehicle is distinctly not.

When the itinerant preacher leaves off the tasteless biblical quotations and begins to spin a parable, however, Dinah immediately drops her knitting to listen to the story. The preacher tells of a beautiful princess whose husband, after lavishing gifts and affection on her, leaves her without granting her a divorce, so that she remains legally anchored, as the word *agunah* implies [*ogen* = anchor], to an absent man. The preacher expounds the parable's allegorical description of the relationship between Israel, lost in the darkness of exile, and God, her distant, rejecting husband, but Dinah remains transfixed at the literal level of the story, wondering until late into the night what happened to the princess. Looking out at the dark night, she remembers how the preacher spoke of the "darkness of exile." Finally, she turns to her husband across the dark and dank bedroom.

> —Raphael—she stretches a gaunt hand through the air—You understood him, there, in the synagogue: What happened to her? What happened to the *agunah*? Did he come back to her, the husband? Did he come back?
> There is no reply. He, the old man, is not asleep, but he does not answer.
> —That's the way it always is—she shakes her head, as it were, to the wondrous princess, intimating to the princess what she thinks about "them," men, and then she turns over again and faces the wall, the window.[32]

Dinah's situation is truly that of the agunah, even though she technically has a husband. She is dependent on him even to understand the meaning of her own situation, a meaning he withholds in a form of intellectual abandonment. Baron's reading of Dinah's literalist "misreading" of the parable is a double one. On one hand, Dinah's mistake is duly noted, and the implied author marks her own ironic distance from the woman schooled to hear only "stories."[33] More than that, the implied author echoes the hermeneutic mode of the preacher by having the title refer to both the princess in the parable and, indirectly, to Dinah, whose unhappy marriage could be compared to the abandonment/dependence of the abandoned wife. That is, Baron's story is also a kind of midrash, also a multilayered performance of a Hebrew text, though it takes a different turn from the familiar allegorical interpretation of the preacher. The woman writer's affiliations are with the preacher she describes and criticizes, much more than with the female protagonist for whose experience she evinces such empathy.

On the other hand, by returning the parable to the specific situation of women, the narrator, like Dinah, resists the long tradition, in which the preacher firmly stands, of reading the sexual conflict in potentially subversive texts such as the Song of Songs as metaphorically describing God's relation with the Jewish people. The new midrash, in the final analysis, is an aggregate of Dinah's "misreading" by ignorance and the implied author's rereading of this misreading as an act of resistance. Together, the two readers privilege the literal over the allegorical, the female over the male perspective, and the darkness of the sociopolitical exile of women over the national tragedy of the Jewish diaspora. Dinah's marginal position is transformed into a powerful textual maneuver that can strip traditional texts of their old, set meanings. The Hebrew secular modernism that rescues sacred texts from allegorical readings is rediscovered in this story in an unexpected place—in the traditional Jewish woman's ignorance of, or freedom from, the accretions of masculinist hermeneutics.[34]

Baron's story is aimed not only at traditional masculine hermeneutics but also at least one of the modernist varieties. Sh. Y. Agnon's "Agunot" (Abandoned Wives), which first appeared in 1908, has a nearly identical title, a female protagonist also named Dinah, and a similar interest in midrash. As in Baron's story, there are no actually abandoned wives in "Agunot," nor, in fact, does the word even appear. Agnon's story is set wholly within a traditional world, just as it makes a quasi-traditional use of the lover-beloved paradigm to suggest relationships between men and women, God and the Jewish people, Israel and the Diaspora. In his distinctively modernist approach to tradition, Agnon activates all these levels simultaneously rather than use the human love relationship to tell the national story. Altogether missing from Agnon's narrative is a consciousness of the power imbalances between men and women. The imbalances are there, in Dinah's forced seclusion, described in the traditional terms as the feminine modesty "all the honor of the princess is within," Ps. 45:14); but her "purity" and "modesty" are formulaic praises of the traditional woman, not occasions for social protest. The tragedy of the story is not Dinah's imprisonment but her inability to unite with her perfect mate. This is not seen as a particularly feminine problem, since it is one she shares with the man her father chose for her. Dinah and her new husband, Yechezkel, are sexually and emotionally estranged from each other, but each has his or her own lost love: their situations are irreconcilable but nonetheless reflections of each other. Agnon's language captures this terrible symmetry.

He sat in one corner and his thoughts were elsewhere and she sat in a different corner and her thoughts were elsewhere. His thoughts wandered to his father's house, where Freydele's mother, the neighbor, had served them since his mother died. Dinah's thoughts wandered to the Ark and the artist who crafted it, who had disappeared in the city and nobody knew where he had gone.[35]

The legal asymmetry inscribed in the very word *agunah* is lost in Agnon's translation of the term to describe all mismatched and lost souls, male and female. It would be wrong to imply that Agnon's story contains no social critique: he argues against the tragic effects of arranged marriages and a class bias that fails to appreciate the artisan class. But where Agnon pluralizes the term "agunot," using it as a code for a more general social as well as existential condition, and even derives a masculine version of the term to adopt as his own name, Baron's version returns the term "agunah" to the singular, to women, and to the phenomenology of the lone female listener at a male discursive event.[36]

III

Much of Baron's work engages the Hebrew canon in an intertextual dialogue, although it does so from the "feminine" margins. But Baron also wrote stories that openly allude to and incorporate "women's" Yiddish religious literature. Like Abramovitsh, Baron acknowledges a literary matrilineage as well as patrilineage.

Baron dealt with the feminine Yiddish tradition most explicitly in her earlier work. In these stories, Baron rarely quotes directly from these texts, as Abramovitsh did (rather late in his career) in his description of Sarah's personal prayer and as Baron commonly does with Hebrew intertexts. Rather, Baron presents Yiddish woman's texts materially, as tattered or yellowed books, signifying by their poor condition the relative status of women in the social order. There is a long Jewish tradition of correspondences between bodies and texts; for example, the Torah scroll wears a "cloak," it is ritually kissed and embraced, it is buried if damaged, the Torah pointer is a "hand," a man who recites the blessing over the Torah in a synagogue is called "a bridegroom of the Torah." Baron's innovation is to turn this tradition toward women's texts, and to use it in the services of a feminist critique.

Baron wrote two stories entitled "Genizah" (Burial); the first appeared in 1908 and the other fourteen years later. Both stories describe the ritual practice of burying sacred books or pages that have been torn or otherwise damaged, partly to ensure their afterlife when the dead arise in the Messianic era. The 1908 story describes the ritual of burying damaged sacred books from the perspective of a young girl, the daughter of the town rabbi who is organizing the ritual. While her father allows her to participate to a limited extent in preparing for the burial, her older brother takes the opportunity to ridicule her and mock the "women's books" her mother wants included in the burial. Throughout, the narrative draws parallels between the physical life of books and the textually dictated life of the town. In an early scene, the narrator describes the rabbi's tender, nearly erotic love for the damaged Torah scroll he carries to the cemetery.

Daddy takes a few steps, goes over to the sexton, bends his head and kisses the Torah. Carefully, carefully he takes it [her] from the sexton, carefully he takes it in his arms and he clasps it very close to his heart and again kisses it. . . .

So too does a mother embrace her only son, when he finally falls asleep, and even though she doesn't want to disturb his sleep, she still kisses him softly, kisses him anyway and embraces him!

The rabbi's embrace of the Torah scroll stands in sharp contrast to the ritual treatment of women's literature, in other words, with the Yiddish literature that was metonymically connected to its female audience rather than, like the Torah, metaphorically associated with an idealized feminine figure. The narrator's brother prevents her from including her mother's "tear-stained" collection of Yiddish personal prayers (the tkhine) among the Hebrew religious books to be buried, calling it a "rag" and tossing it aside. The exclusion of this book is echoed by the call of the men as they walk to the cemetery: "Women out of the way!" At the burial ceremony, the narrator, seeing her mother mournfully looking for her beloved book of prayers among the other books, runs home to find it.

Here is the *tkhine*. It [or she, since *tkhine* is feminine in Hebrew] had been flung in the corner, its pages scattered, its yellow stains so noticeable. . . . I grab it and run back to the cemetery. And here—Daddy is still standing, his face pale, his eyes damp and his lips moving.

And I'm next to the open grave:

—t-z-z-z-z!!

That's how the pages of the prayer book whisper to me when they touch the other old books in the grave.

And it seems to me that these old books, addressing the poor prayer book with hostility, say these harsh words:

—r-r-a-a-g-g! Get out of here! . . .

In another moment my brother will approach, peering into the grave, casting an angry look at me, and take the book and throw it far, far away.

A sharp pain stabs my heart; my brain reels . . . the trees are dancing to greet me, standing around me and swaying and singing and dancing. . . . And I too begin to dance, but my legs stumble a little and I drop to the ground . . .

*   *   *37

The books themselves reenact, in the little girl's imagination, the hierarchical segregation of the social order. When the "masculine" books call the collection of Yiddish women's prayers a "rag" and order it out of the grave, they speak the words of an exorcism ritual, "Get out of here!" The presence of the "feminine" book within the grave is not only legally unsanctioned, it also represents the monstrous threat of a dybbuk. In including this otherworldly dimension, Baron suggests that the men and their texts are not only loath to share a space with women and their texts, they are also afraid of being "possessed" by the feminine realm that always threatens to encroach. And the subcanonical romances or "smutty" literature so often associated with women readers were also commonly called rags.

The little girl's identification with the book is reinforced by the similarity in their fates. The narrator's fainting (marked by the three asterisks) at the open grave doubly imitates the burial of the book: in falling to the ground she reenacts its burial, and her loss of consciousness during the ceremony marks the absence of female rituals of memory and the erasure of feminine tradition. Yet the gap in this story produces a stronger feminist text than the burial of the women's book would have done. *Genizah*, in the context of the story, means "the burial of sacred texts," but it more literally means "concealment." Just as the story takes full advantage of the ambiguous link between discarding and burying, it also plays with both senses of its title. In refraining from resolving the story and showing us what happened to the Yiddish book, Baron allows its fate to hover between rejection and redemption through burial, sanctioned concealment or shameful exposure, and suggests that the two possibilities are paradoxically related.

It is worth noting that the story, with its explicit feminist rage, is dedicated "to the memory of my father's soul." The story appeared, in fact, thirty days after the death of Baron's father, the day traditionally marked by a memorial service at the graveside. "Burial," then, is a meditation on the powerful links between burying and honoring, between words and bodies. But it also reinscribes, under the signature of the writer-daughter, the authority to decide who will memorialize the past and whose past should be memorialized. In insisting on including the Yiddish women's book in a male ritual and a Hebrew story, Baron poses the problem of female transmission within a system governed by men and male texts.

The 1922 "Burial" describes the ceremony through an omniscient narrator, in a measured and distanced, almost ethnographic, tone. The anger against the unequal treatment of men and women, women's texts and men's, that dominates the 1908 story is barely detectable here, and then only in a single passage. Mina, an old woman "from the house of priests," has some difficulty adding her torn copy of the *Tsenerene*, the women's Bible, to the pile, not because anyone is trying to stop her but mostly because she is old and the young boys are too absorbed in their playing with the town billy goat to let her pass through. The rabbi of the town sees her frustration and, conscious of her distinguished (and patrilineal) pedigree, graciously accepts her offering, mentally comparing her to the woman whose meager sacrificial Temple offering the priest defended, saying, "Do not mock her, it is as if she were offering her soul." The priestly ties of the woman are symbolically transferred to him by the force of his grounding in the texts—whatever they say about the importance of her lineage, he is the one who knows what they say.

The second "Burial" does continue to think through the relations between sex, or body, and text. In one passage, the rabbi catches himself thinking about his Torah sermon while still undressed after his ritual immersion, "despite the inappropriateness of the place." An elaborate and humorous parallel is drawn between the rabbi's naked body and the Torah scroll (here grammatically masculine, since it is referred to as a "sefer Torah," a Torah scroll) in the scene that follows, when the rabbi and his sexton remove the torn scroll from the attic of the synagogue.

Suddenly the sexton reeled back from the chest in the corner and cried:
—But it's [he's] naked, rabbi!
—Who is? the rabbi asked in surprise, without recognizing his own voice, which had no echo here.
—The holy book! The sexton set his candle down on the chest where the little Torah scroll lay naked, without a cloth or covering, and the rabbi, still carefully holding "The Tree of Life," tucked it [him] with a father's compassion beneath the corners of his coat, and with great emotion made his way carefully down the ladder.

The irreverent joke that connects the uncovered Torah scroll and the unclothed rabbi remains in the masculine sphere (including the sexton who is the only witness to the scene). The masculine sphere of textual study, as in Abramovitsh's description of the Hebrew writers' circle, remains undisturbed by the presence of either a biological or metaphorical female.

The two stories named "Burial" demonstrate Baron's movement from a female-centered narrative with a female narrator to an omniscient narrator's metaphysical and democratic view of Jewish tradition. Rather than being organized around a gap, the burial ritual ends with a redemptive vision of four hundred years of shtetl residents, of all classes and both genders, rising from their graves at the end of days. The development that can be traced between the two stories is symptomatic of the general course of Baron's writing career over fifty years. Govrin describes this literary and biographical progression as a movement from openness, political activity, and explicit feminist protest to concealment, self-enclosure, and a poetics of indirection and moderation. She traces Baron's evolution into "a legend in her own time, a legendary princess who voluntarily imprisoned herself in her house, granting few people permission to visit her, and embroidering stories about a vanished world in her solitude, while maintaining a living presence that transcended space and time."[38]

The two stories record the dialectic of enclosure and disclosure, burial and resurrection, but they demonstrate that this dialectic came to be weighted against disclosure. Baron failed to include the earlier stories (including the first "Burial") in her collections, calling them "rags." In her biographical notes, Baron's daughter, Tsipora Aharonovitsh, describes her mother's process of circumscribing and fixing the canon of her own works.

This is the time to comment on D.B.'s [sic] denigrating and belittling attitude toward all the stories she wrote in her youth, which she called "rags."

She forcefully resisted the publication of any story or fragment from those days, and on a list she made of all her stories, in order of their appearance, she wrote in a few places, as if as a testimony for posterity, the word *psulim* [defective, flawed, or disqualified].[39]

"Rags," echoing as it does the masculine assessment of the collection of Yiddish women's prayers in the first "Burial," could signal the growing discomfort of a woman writer with her own proximity to feminine traditions and the distance of the later writer from these traditions. But we can also read Baron's calling her earliest stories rags as more evidence of her self-irony, not her self-denigration at all. Rags, after all, aside from their domestic usefulness, are often the raw material of women's *bricolage*, to reclaim Claude Lévi-Strauss's term for the female crafts. Baron's reworking of earlier material in her later work may be the perfect example of this feminine ingenuity in creating art from the discarded and outworn. Moreover, Baron's work shows strong affiliations with "rag" literature (ghost stories, pornography, children's stories, memoirs, sentimental or romance fiction).

The second word Baron used in assessing her early work, *psulim*, moves even more clearly in two directions. While Baron seems to dismiss her early work in the language of rabbinic legal decisions, her words read differently when we remember the uses to which she put that very term. In the context of the two "Burials," the "defective" or "flawed" books or other ritual objects are still holy, and their burial is a mark of love and respect. And not only do these damaged texts hold an honored place in Baron's stories, the narrative describes the burial as designed to assure their afterlife. Perhaps we are meant to see that Baron transmitted her early stories by burying them, as it were, in the reworked stories that appear in the later collections. In any case, Baron herself is the best teacher of the value of the fragmentary, the apparently damaged, and the nearly lost.

IV

On Abramovitsh's famous "triumphal tour" in the summer of 1909, the writer Zrubavel tells us, the Vilna writers and cultural activists decided to take group photographs with him as "a memento for generations to come." The Hebrew and Yiddish writers were photographed separately; Zrubavel describes the event from the perspective of the Yiddish writers, of which he was one.

Yiddish writers with D. Baron and Abramovitsh (at center).

We decided to meet at the photographer very early in the morning, an hour before the "grandfather" had to leave for Warsaw.

Not everyone showed up on time. Some, I don't remember who they were, were late and were left out. But we made a gentlemanly gesture toward the one "lady" in our midst and persuaded the photographer to photograph her separately and put her into the group photograph. We left a place reserved for that purpose. We did it out of love and care for our colleague, the writer Dvora Baron, who by then had already acquired a place of honor in our literature. By the way, she also had a lot of personal charm, and we all respected her for her knowledge, of religious sources as well.[40]

Despite the fact that she wrote many more Hebrew stories, despite the enthusiastic interest she aroused as a Hebrew writer, it was the Yiddish writers rather than the Hebrew ones who left room for Baron's photograph to be inserted into their group portrait (see figs. 5 and 6). Baron's work was eventually canonized as (a marginal) part of Hebrew literature; but the 1908 photographic self-canonization of the Hebrew and Yiddish writers of Vilna suggests that her place would have been more easily established in the other camp.

The biographical notes assembled after her death give us the tantalizing information that Baron's first work, written at the age of seven, was a play in Yiddish: "D.B. could not say anything about the nature of

Hebrew writers with Abramovitsh.

this play, other than that the names of its heroes and the plot were taken from the love stories her older sister would read in Yiddish. By the age of twelve she was already writing Hebrew stories."[41] The passage suggests that Baron's move to Hebrew from Yiddish was early and firmly established. Nevertheless, Baron would always be associated with Yiddish, because of her gender and interest in "women's themes" and traditional women's culture and because she situated her stories in a Yiddish-speaking environment.

Dvora Baron came to prominence in a literary atmosphere that was reaping the benefits of Abramovitsh's projects of modernizing Hebrew and raising the stature of Yiddish literature. Partly because both literatures had such a worthy "grandfather" in Abramovitsh, Hebrew and Yiddish writers in the first decades of this century could command similar respect among their audiences. Nevertheless, the growing politicization and polarization of the Hebrew and Yiddish camps, with the rise of linguistic-political ideologies like Zionism and Socialism, created new obstacles in the path of the writer who failed to make a clear choice of a literary language.[42] As was the case among others of her literary generation, Baron's early Yiddish writings—along with the early Hebrew stories—were left out of the collections in which her work found a wide public. But while her precocious career as a teenage Hebrew writer is a central part of the Baron legend, her not inconsiderable investment in Yiddish literature (eleven short stories in Yiddish, five of them translations from Hebrew, were published between 1904 and 1912; one, from the Alexandria period—1915–1919—remained unpublished) has been neither incorporated into the biographical narrative nor subjected to critical or popular attention. With the appearance, in 1988, of Nurit Govrin's critical biography and newly collected stories of Baron's first decade of literary production, *The First Half,* a more complete picture of the bilingual Baron can emerge.

Both the Hebrew and the Yiddish stories bear the traces of Baron's struggle to achieve a place in the circle of Hebrew writers. Baron's progression "from exposure to concealment" is symptomatic not only of the movement from earlier to later writing but also of the differences between her early Hebrew and Yiddish writings, though these were written during the same period. The early Hebrew stories, to generalize, combine intellectualized feminist argument with a sexual and emotional reticence; the Yiddish stories, by contrast, are among the most sexually, politically, and stylistically radical in her oeuvre. Given the loose publication standards of the time and medium, it is not always easy to decide how much of the difference between Yiddish and Hebrew versions of some of her stories can be ascribed to the free hand of an editor or even an unnamed translator. And we do not always know when the stories were written, or which version was written first. Nevertheless, these differences reveal certain patterns that would be hard to ascribe to a diverse group of editors and translators.

Let me draw the outlines of these patterns. In a series of stories that appeared between the years 1908 and 1910, during Baron's final years in Europe, Baron dealt directly and explicitly with feminist themes. These stories include "Kadisha/Kadish," "Sister," "Burial," "An Only Daughter," and "Grandma Henya."[43] These stories argue for women's participation in Torah study, expose the mistreatment of women's texts, insist on women's entitlement in ritually memorializing the dead, and explore the place of daughters in the patriarchal family. A few of these motifs reappear in later stories, although they find less extreme expression there. Clearly, these early texts are central to any feminist analysis of Baron's work.

Baron's feminist thematics has two strands: the exclusion of women and women's books from equal participation in religious and family life; and the sexual rivalries, ambivalences, and tensions between men and women, and older and younger generations, in the patriarchal family. It is this second strand that is more prominent in the Yiddish stories, suggesting their affiliation with a different genre than the Hebrew stories; while the Hebrew stories are generically linked to the realist literature of social protest, the Yiddish stories are closer to expressionism, or, more specifically, to the gothic family tale. Sibling rivalry reaches murderous levels and intergenerational family love approaches incest in Yiddish stories like "An Only Daughter," "Kaddish," and "Grandma Henya," while the Hebrew stories "Sister," "Kadisha," and "Grandma Henya" transmute or sublimate these tensions into a more moderate psychological realism. Moreover, two and perhaps three Yiddish stories mentioned here involve the return of the dead (in "An Only Daughter," the "dead" returns in the sense that, after the older sister's murder of her younger sister is averted, the older girl feels her sister's continued existence to be uncanny). Such otherworldly and grotesque effects are otherwise absent from Baron's work.

The Hebrew "Sister" and the Yiddish "An Only Daughter" both describe the reactions of an older sister to the birth of a new daughter in the family. "Sister," however, emphasizes the disappointment over the birth of yet another girl into a family of four daughters, a disappointment that is compared to the joy, decades earlier, that followed upon the birth of their father, an only son. The disappointment is so deep that the family ignores the new baby, not bothering to name her, and the anguished mother accidentally drops the infant. In the final paragraphs the narrator, the oldest sister, lifts the crying infant: "Sh-sh-sh, my little one, sh-sh-sh, my baby, sh-sh-sh, my sister, there, aren't you my sister now, my sis-ss-ter." The narrator's acceptance of her new sister stands in contrast to her own earlier coldness toward both the new baby girl and the other women in the family: "No—my heart is not moved by mother's weeping. My sisters' and aunts' weeping don't touch my heart—after all, they're only women . . . it's my mother who's responsible for all this." And when she hears the baby crying, her words are chillingly double-edged: "This miserable little creature—how can I quiet her . . . ?"[44]

The malevolence that threatens to break out into the open in the Hebrew "Sister," and that is finally overcome at the conclusion of the story, takes center stage and approaches the homicidal in the Yiddish "An Only Daughter." The birth of a new daughter in this story is, from the outset, a deathly occurrence. The narrator, listening to her grandmother tease her about her overthrown status as an only child, "sees before her—like an open grave—Grandmother's toothless mouth." And the baby's wide-open mouth reminds the narrator of a neighbor woman who also once had "a small red-faced creature, and one day his own mother fell asleep on him and the next day they took him out of the house and never brought him back."[45] The fate of the neighbor's child gives the young narrator the idea of strangling her sister; the murder is averted only because, in the darkness, she mistakes the family cat for the infant.

"Grandma Henya" also becomes more macabre in the move from the Hebrew to the Yiddish version. In the Hebrew, the gossip explains Henya's mysterious appearance in town as the result of her having accidentally and grotesquely killed her child, like the neighbor woman in "An Only Daughter."

Her husband died and left her many goods and a single infant. One night, when her young son was in bed with her, his small body got stuck underneath hers. His cries were in vain, his convulsions and quivering were in vain—his mother was fast asleep and didn't feel a thing. The next day she found him dead, with thick, warm blood flowing and seeping from his mouth.[46]

The Yiddish version, by contrast, hints darkly at a connection between the father's death and the mother's taking near-incestuous comfort in her son. Here, the scene is triangulated into an Oedipal struggle among three family members, one of whom is a ghost.

A terrible misfortune happened to her: on the day her first son was born, her husband died. She bathed the child in her tears, wrapped him in her own hair and loved him enough for two. One night, however, when she was lying in bed with her child and taking too much pleasure with him, a deadly sleep came down upon her from heaven. Her husband appeared to her from the grave and begged her:

"Wake up from your sleep and see what you are doing with our child—you are strangling him with your own hands . . . "

She heard his words, but was unable to move. And when she woke up from her sleep the next morning, she found a bloody corpse in bed with her.[47]

Both stories present two versions of Henya's arrival in town, the second of which also involves a transgression: the gossips report that Henya was overly involved in the Torah study of her husband and seven sons. The hardworking mother, they say, would proudly eavesdrop on her family's Torah study from the women's section of the synagogue. In the Hebrew:

She would gaze and feel proud, look and enjoy. And this enjoyment did not find favor with the One who spoke and the world came into being. A fire blazed down from heaven and set the study hall on fire while the eight souls were still within it. In a few days Grandmother Henya accompanied a wagon loaded down with bones. They were her husband's and sons' scorched bones.[48]

The Yiddish version of this same scene adds a few elements to the narrative.

She would gaze and feel delight, look and take pride in herself:
—That is my husband . . . those are my children . . .
Her proud words were not pleasing, as it were, before the Highest One, so a fire came down from the sky and burned the holy house, while all the eight souls were still between its high walls. The next morning the wife and mother picked out the scorched bones with her own hands.[49]

In the Yiddish, Henya's pleasure in her family's Torah study is explicitly described as threatening the hierarchical social and even divine order. Her pride is not only in the diligence of her husband and sons but also in her own role as wife and mother, expressed as a sense of ownership. This connection is repeated in the grisly punishment, which links her to what is left of these male bodies more intimately than the Hebrew narrative, where she accompanies the wagon. Moreover, God's anger is a kind of jealousy, not so much over her partial invasion of the male sphere as over her self-assertion of a quasi-divine (pro)creator of these men. The female transgression, then, moves from intellectual hubris in the Hebrew to sexual rivalry in the Yiddish.

The two versions of "Kaddish" follow the pattern of Henya's accidental/sexual murder of her child, where the Yiddish introduces the supernatural and macabre to expose psychosexual tensions concealed in the Hebrew. The stories represent Baron's most explicit exploration of women's unequal relations to the Jewish liturgy, in this case, the kaddish prayer. In both stories, the young narrator and protagonist insists on saying kaddish for her beloved grandfather, who left no male heir, although this prayer is traditionally recited by men. In the Yiddish, though, the congregants block her approach to the altar and her desire is diverted by an encounter with her dead grandfather.

Looking at me from above, from the sacred Ark, I see two pious-clear eyes: "Child, child . . . " so sorrowfully, so beseechingly, "child, child." And I see how the flames of the yahrzeit candle flow like an enormous burning sea, embracing me completely, completely.[50]

This scene is entirely absent in the Hebrew, where the young girl succeeds in saying the prayer. Her success is mirrored in the title of the Hebrew story, "Kadisha," where the writer reclaims the Hebrew word by creating a grammatically feminine form from it. The Hebrew narrative simply describes the triumphant entry of a little girl into the men's section of the beit midrash.

Many pairs of eyes penetrated me as I entered the synagogue. Everyone stared at me in amazement. For a moment I hesitated; my dress was so white among all the black caftans. But here I was already beside the pulpit:
  "yitgadal veyitkadash shmey raba"
  My heart pounded furiously—
When I emerged from the synagogue, a group of boys surrounded me, all of them pointing:
  "It's 'her' . . . 'kadisha' . . . ha, ha, ha."[51]

  "Kaddish," by contrast, is something more or less than a "feminist" story. It tells a complex narrative about the inextricability of the present and past, represented by the girl and her grandfather, and the irresolvable desires of each of the partners in this dance of opposites that even death cannot put to rest. The scene in the Hebrew version that most graphically describes the hierarchical gender order against which the young girl struggles, in which the young boys of the town refuse to allow the girls to climb up a small hill they call Mount Sinai, is absent from the Yiddish version. Indeed such a scene would be out of place in a story whose lines of tension are strongest between family members. The Yiddish mentions the dead grandmother, whose silent absorption in her husband's nighttime Torah study is reflected in her granddaughter's similar fascination. The suggestion is made that the young girl serves as a substitute for the dead wife, raising the stakes in the relationship between the old man and his granddaughter. Even nature is implicated in the family drama. The Yiddish version ends with the girl sitting outside, "and around, like an angry stepmother, the still, black night."
  The ambivalent relationships at the heart of the Yiddish story barely appear in the Hebrew. In "Kadisha," the grandfather arranged lessons for his granddaughter and delights in her progress. In "Kaddish," the young girl pays for her own lessons on the sly and demands that her grandfather "test" (farher—the term is loaded with the agonistic atmosphere common to the masculine sphere of Talmud study) her knowledge. When she proceeds to recite the kaddish, her accomplishment seems less a matter of feminine entitlement than the frightening hubris of the young toward their elders. The narrator stands at an ironic distance from the girl's achievement, describing how she pushes the prayer book away and recites "with eyes piously closed."
  The Yiddish, in other words, brings to the surface what is implicit in the vernacular use of the term "kaddish" to refer to a son who will recite

the prayer for the dead parent. The relation between generations cannot but be fraught with an awareness that offspring represent not only continued existence but also substitution and death. For the young girl to accomplish her desire and recite the kaddish, her grandfather must pass away, and her reaction to his death is chillingly off the point: "But what did it have to do with me? If I only had a black dress, a completely black dress, I would be a lot more like a boy, a lot more." And the grandfather's ghostly appearance as a sorrowful but rebuking angel, in the place of honor in the men's section, suggests his continued participation in the rivalry between men and women, young and old, the still alive and the already dead.

It is not coincidental, I think, that these tensions are explored in Baron's Yiddish work rather than in the Hebrew. The macabre and the supernatural are more closely associated with Yiddish literature and folk culture than with the Hebrew literary canon, although they find their place in Hebrew as well. In Baron's Yiddish stories, however, the grotesque is used not only to elucidate psychological currents concealed in the Hebrew. The differences between the two bodies of work may also be an oblique reflection of and commentary on the different trajectories of modern Hebrew and Yiddish literature. In Yiddish prose the dead return to have their say; Hebrew is the jumping-off point where the present leaves the past behind.

But there is another possible reading of the patterns I have outlined. Yiddish provided Baron with a more open arena for an exploration of the life of the body than Hebrew did. Baron's mind and voice called over the masculine sphere of Hebrew, but the woman's body had no place there. Only in the darkness of the "women's section" of her Yiddish production could the dramas of incest and parent-child murder unfold. If Baron's later stories are models of artistic modulation and control, it is the Yiddish stories and the earlier Hebrew stories that can show us some of what it was that came under Baron's control.

The fascination with Dvora Baron in the later years of her life and after her death can be traced, in part, to the mythology that arose around Baron's self-imposed isolation in the heart of Tel Aviv, and to the curious way this self-concealment combined with her continuing immersion in a fictional world associated with her distant childhood. The drama of Baron's life, then, arose from this split between her present "real" surroundings and the "fictional" past from which she derived her sustenance. My aim in ending with the legend of Baron's later years is not to question the validity of this myth but rather to note how closely its structure is foreshadowed in the early stories, written during years when no one could mistake her for an eccentric recluse. One can read the transformation of Baron into a "legendary princess who voluntarily imprisoned herself in her house . . . [yet] maintained a living presence that transcended space and time" as a further development of the split arena—epistemological, psychological, and linguistic—that characterized her work from the start. From this point of view, Baron's literary self-exposure/physical self-concealment provides an appropriate context for her work. As in the first version of "Burial," concealment exists in powerful dialectic with the drive toward memory. But one can also imagine the mythical qualities of Baron's biography as yet another of her literary creations, a cousin to the abandoned princess in "Agunah." As readers of Baron's myth, like Dinah and her husband, where we sit determines how we understand her story.

4 A Stormy Divorce

The Sexual Politics of the
Hebrew-Yiddish "Language War"

Eliezer Ben-Yehuda,
What a far-out kind of Jew.
Words, words, words, words,
He concocted in his feverish brain.

And he had a son, and thus said he:
My firstborn shall be called Ben-Yehuda, Itamar
From the breast until old age,
From circumcision until the grave—
He will be a sworn friend to the Hebrew tongue,
And a fierce foe of all foreign ones.
Itamar—became a man,
Tall as a palm and handsome,
And he spoke the Hebrew tongue.
Itamar Ben-Avi,
His father's prophecy,
The sort of man who suits me.
                —"Eliezer Ben-Yehuda," lyrics by Yaron London

I want our son Eri to know Hebrew well. All other decisions I
leave to you.
                —Zev Jabotinsky, 1918 letter/will to his wife

I

In the past few decades, critics and historians have begun to contest and reevaluate the centrality of Eliezer Ben-Yehuda's role in the revival of spoken Hebrew.[1] These critics argue, either explicitly or implicitly, that the Hebrew revival actually occurred both much earlier and much later than the 1880s and 1890s, when Ben-Yehuda was attempting to realize his project of raising a child to speak solely Hebrew. That is, Hebrew, or Loshn-koydesh, was occasionally spoken in the centuries before the revival, by members of different Jewish communities who shared no other language or by fervent Jews who wished to sanctify the Sabbath by speaking only the Holy Tongue. Moreover, the work of writers like Abramovitsh, whose Yiddish-inflected style infused written Hebrew with the idiomatic flexibility it had sorely lacked, had already set the stage for a full-blown vernacular revival years before Ben-Yehuda's project was launched.

Nevertheless, neither the scattered episodes of Hebrew speech nor the fluency of Abramovitsh's Hebrew style directly produced a Hebrew-speaking environment, and Ben-Yehuda's experiment was no more successful. Hebrew finally did begin to become the vernacular of an entire society only during the Second Aliya (the wave of immigration that began in 1905 and lasted until 1914), under very different circumstances than Ben-Yehuda's isolated work in Jerusalem in the 1880s. Benjamin Harshav is perhaps most responsible for the demystification of what has become an article of faith in Israel, Ben-Yehuda's "revival" of the Hebrew tongue. Harshav's revisionary linguistic history of the yishuv (which parallels recent historical approaches to many other aspects of *yishuv*, or pre-Statehood, history) insists that, "in spite of his pathetic figure and life, Ben-Yehuda had no real influence on the revival itself, which began to strike roots about twenty-five years after his arrival in Erets-Israel, in the milieu created by the Second Aliya.[2] Whatever one makes of his actual function in the Hebrew revival, however, it would be impossible to deny the other part of Harshav's claim: that Ben-Yehuda's position vis-à-vis modern Hebrew has attained the status of popular national mythology.

The process of mythologizing Ben-Yehuda's career begins with his own writings. In his autobiography, Ben-Yehuda describes the circumstances surrounding the birth of his son in the hushed tone of a witness to a miracle.

On the fifteenth of Av, the first new settlement of the yishuv was founded, the settlement of Rishon-letsiyon; on that very day, in a dark corner of a small room close to the Temple Mount, the child was born with whom the first experiment of reviving Hebrew as a spoken tongue was supposed to commence. . . . Is it not one of the wondrous events of human history that the beginning of the revival of our land, if one can call it that, and the beginning of the revival of our language happened simultaneously, on the same day, virtually at the same hour? On the day that the first settlement of the nation that had decided to return to the soil of their fathers was founded in the land of the fathers, on that very day was born the son who was destined to be the first of the children of the nation who would return to speaking the language of the fathers.[3]

The magical quality of the birth of the first Hebrew child is heightened, in Ben-Yehuda's account, by the child's appearance, as it were, ex nihilo, an effect achieved partially by the mother's absence from the narrative. The birth is translated from the natural universe not only to the realm of miracles but also to the historical sphere, one dominated by fathers, the fatherland, and the language of the father. The word "fathers" (*avot*) is repeated three times in the last line cited above, in "land of the fathers," "country of the fathers," and "language of the fathers"—avoiding the myriad feminine *topoi* for describing Zion and the Land of Israel. The word, of course, could also be translated as "ancestors," but there are other elements of Ben-Yehuda's narrative that suggest the centrality of paternity to his Hebraist-Zionist project.

In describing Ben-Yehuda's place in the pantheon of Zionist heroes, Harshav conveys his sense that the myth of the Hebrew revival is inextricable from Ben-Yehuda's role as a father.

> Popular mythology feeds off of the image of a hero who personifies an idea, the individual who in his personal life, which is understood by all, and especially in his suffering and sacrifice, is a symbol of the exalted goal. Thus Herzl is constructed as a legendary king (although "Hibat Zion" preceded him); Bialik as the poet-prophet, who paid with his "blood and fat" for the blaze his verses struck in the people (although there were other first-rate poets among his peers, such as Tshernikhovsky and Steinberg); Trumpeldor as "the one-armed hero" (although he lost his hand defending Russia from the Japanese); Brenner as the personification of the "in-spite-of-it-all" (as if his assassination at the hands of Arab rioters justifies the despair in his writings); and Eliezer Ben-Yehuda as the father of the Hebrew revival, who sacrificed his family on its altar.[4]

Harshav intends his catalog to demonstrate the condensation and distortion by which the idiosyncrasies of individual life stories are remade in the broad shapes of national ideals. Thus, the single-mindedness of Ben-Yehuda's lonely endeavor, his planting linguistic seeds in what could not have been very fertile ground, could legitimize his title "father of the Hebrew revival." And Ben-Yehuda's paternal role is not just a figure of speech. In account after account, the varied scope of Ben-Yehuda's linguistic experiment is primarily reduced to and expressed by his activities as father, rather than as editor, publisher, inventor of new words (or as his detractors would have it, manager of the Hebrew "word factory"), or founder of various language societies.

Ben-Yehuda's story differs from Harshav's other examples, however, because his heroism is both derived from and qualified by his fatherhood: popular mythological reworkings of Ben-Yehuda's career demonstrate the centrality of the family drama to the Hebrew revival and the degree to which this drama is touched with the psychological and ethical ambiguities of patriarchal (self-)sacrifice.[5] And while other stories about national heroes typically suppress the less attractive characteristics of their subjects, Ben-Yehuda's problematic fatherly behavior almost always has a central part in the cultural texts that transmit his story. Rather than elide Ben-Yehuda's "sacrifice" of his family, popular biographies, children's books, critical histories, and so on, cite his zealotry and its domestic effects as further proof of Ben-Yehuda's laudably unswerving commitment to Hebrew, an enhancement rather than a diminution of his heroic stature. What emerges in these narratives is a fable as morally complex as the binding of Isaac, an intertext to which Harshav's description of Ben-Yehuda's "sacrifice" of his family "on the altar" indirectly refers.

My aim here, however, is not to judge either Ben-Yehuda's character or his role in the Hebrew revival, or to decide whether Ben-Yehuda's family troubles were the price he paid or exacted for the vernacularization of Hebrew. Rather, I examine the insistence with which the story of the revival of the Hebrew vernacular has been transmitted as a story about the conflicting claims of Jewish paternity and maternity, about the establishment of masculine control over areas of Jewish life traditionally in the hands of women, and about domestic difficulty and guilt. The stories that have arisen around the figure of Ben-Yehuda, I argue, have the cultural power they have because they reflect and reinforce basic conflicts of Hebrew and Erets-Israeli society during the interwar period in which these myths began to circulate. Ben-Yehuda's family troubles and language obsession in fact encode and condense the overlapping territories of the language conflict and gender ideologies of his own time and of later times.

Let me draw the outlines of a few versions of what could be called the "primal scene" or the founding myth of the revival of Hebrew as a living tongue. In Ottoman Jerusalem of the 1880s, Eliezer Ben-Yehuda, by supreme linguistic and ideological determination, raised the first native Hebrew speaker in modern times, his son Ben-Tsiyon (later Itamar). The experiment involved creating a "pure" Hebrew environment, severely restricting the child's access to other languages while immersing him in Hebrew speech. Ben-Yehuda relates that he taught his wife Hebrew quickly, even though this task "was a little hard at first." He goes on to explain this difficulty: "As with virtually all Jewish women, and everyone except for a few maskilim and Hebrew writers of the day, even this daughter of the maskil Sh. N. Yonas knew no Hebrew, although she could read the Hebrew letters and write Yiddish."[6]

Most historians seem to agree that Dvora Ben-Yehuda learned Hebrew slowly, if at all. In having a willing wife, Ben-Yehuda was luckier than at least one of the members of the Jerusalem group who had sworn allegiance to his project. As Ben-Yehuda reports, "Arye Horwitz would argue with his wife incessantly because she didn't know Hebrew and didn't have time to learn."[7] Despite the lack of such obvious discord in the Ben-Yehuda household, the difficulties of raising a child in a language one parent could speak only haltingly and the other barely at all seem to have taken their toll. Amos Elon summarizes the domestic manifestations of Ben-Yehuda's project in these words:

Ben-Yehuda's wife knew no Hebrew; while still on shipboard he told her that in Palestine they would speak nothing but Hebrew. He ruthlessly kept his vow. When his first son, Itamar, was born (by a curious coincidence on the same day the colony of Rishon-letsiyon was founded) he became the first child in centuries to hear only Hebrew from both his parents and almost nothing from anyone else, for he was kept isolated from all human contact lest the purity of his Hebrew be spoiled by alien sounds. His mother, though weak and ailing, agreed to her husband's demand not to hire a servant in order that the child might hear nothing but the holy tongue. . . .

It was a risky undertaking. The language was still archaic. Many words indispensable in modern intercourse were missing. The child had no playmates; until his third year he remained almost mute and often refused to utter a word.[8]

In a later passage, Elon recounts that "when Ben-Yehuda's aged mother, who spoke no Hebrew, arrived in Palestine shortly before her death, Ben-Yehuda, who had not seen her for years, refused to talk with her in a language she could understand."[9]

In her biography of Eliezer Ben-Yehuda, Chemda Ben-Yehuda, who was Eliezer's second wife as well as Dvora Ben-Yehuda's younger sister, vividly describes Eliezer standing at the door to the birth chamber and giving the midwife and the female neighbors a Hebrew language exam before he would let them attend the birth; one barren woman, believing she could benefit through sympathetic magic from proximity to the new mother, was allowed to enter—but on the condition that she not call out the prescribed phrase "This is my child," since she could not manage it in Hebrew. Chemda describes Dvora's efforts to silence the excited witness to the birth.

Sheyne Malke sang the infant something with her lips shut. At every moment Sheyne-Malke wanted to say something loving to the newborn child in Zhargon. The mother, however, reminded her of the prohibition against speaking by putting her finger to her lips, and the woman remained silent. After that, we always called her the "dumb aunt" [*hadodah ha'ilemet*].[10]

Chemda also relates that the months after the birth of her child were lonely ones for her sister, although Dvora did not complain. "Mrs. Pines," Chemda writes, "tried to act as mother to Dvora, but since she spoke no Hebrew, she couldn't say much to Dvora in the presence of the newborn."[11]

While Ben-Yehuda writes little about his wife's Hebrew-speaking abilities, some of the passages in his memoir show evidence of a guilty conscience for having sacrificed his wife to the cause; despite Dvora's frail health, Ben-Yehuda writes, he did not allow her a servant girl for fear she would contaminate the pure Hebrew environment, an act of linguistic zealousness he later admitted had been unnecessary. In a long and apologetic passage, Ben-Yehuda describes the factors involved in deciding whether a maidservant would be hired to help the new mother.

The new mother was naturally weak and sickly; poverty, pregnancy, and birth had weakened her further. But even so she willingly and good-naturedly agreed not to have a servant girl in the house, so that the child's ears would hear no sounds other than those of Hebrew. We were afraid of the walls of the house, afraid of the air in the room, lest it absorb the sounds of a foreign tongue emanating from the servant girl, which would enter the child's ears and damage his Hebrew hearing and the Hebrew words would not be absorbed as they should be and the child would not speak Hebrew. This holy soul, who was destined to be the first Hebrew mother of the revival era which would give the nation a Hebrew-speaking generation, took upon herself with love the burden of raising a child without even a little help, although she herself was weak and sickly.[12]

Ben-Yehuda may have been making a reference to any one of these scenarios when he confessed that his determination to speak only Hebrew at times overrode ethical imperatives.

I speak Hebrew, only Hebrew, not only with the members of my household, but even with every man or woman whom I know to more or less understand Hebrew, and I do not take care in this matter to abide by the laws of common respect or courtesy to women [*kibud nashim*]. I act in this with great rudeness, rudeness that has caused many people to hate me and has engendered much opposition to me in Erets-Israel.[13]

If Dvora's Hebrew was limited, her husband's was not much better. One witness to the experiment reported that when Eliezer, for example, wanted Dvora to pour him a cup of coffee with sugar, "he was at a loss to communicate words such as 'cup,' 'saucer,' 'pour,' 'spoon,' and so on. He would say to his wife, in effect: 'Take such and such, and do like so, and bring me this and this, and I will drink' [*k'khi kakh, ve'asi kakh, vehavi'i li kakh, ve'eshteh*]."[14] Under the circumstances, it is not surprising that Itamar Ben-Avi did not speak until he was four, as he relates in his memoirs. His father taught him Hebrew, according to the memoirs of "the First Hebrew Child," primarily by "standing at the crib and reading passages from the Bible to me, so that my ears would grow accustomed to the language."[15] According to Ben-Avi, he spoke his first sentence in the following circumstances: Yehiel Mikhal Pines, a family friend who referred to Ben-Yehuda's experiment as a "modern-day Binding of Isaac," advised Dvora to speak to the child in a language other than Hebrew, for fear the child would grow up to be retarded or mute. She began singing Russian lullabies to him and was caught one day when her husband returned home unexpectedly. As Ben-Avi recounts, Ben-Yehuda was enraged.

"What have you done? All that we've built in the first Hebrew household— you've destroyed in a single day."

Mother tried in vain to defend herself, to place some of the blame on Pines and some on her loneliness and homesickness for the songs she remembered that were so beloved to her.

But with the rage of someone who sees everything he has worked for in ruins, Father pounded his fist on the table—it was a little table, on which he had begun work on the great Hebrew dictionary—and the table smashed into pieces.

"There is no forgiveness for this, Dvora, because you have raised your hand against me and against our eldest son!"

Seeing my father raging and storming, and seeing my mother whimpering like a child who has been caught red-handed—I suddenly understood everything that was happening in this house, stood up straight before my father with the will of a boy defending his mother, even against his father, and screamed, "Father."

Mother covered me with kisses. They both realized that good had emerged from evil, and that from my great shock at seeing my father enraged and my mother sobbing, the dumbness had been removed from my lips and speech had come to my mouth.[16]

Ben-Avi's "real" or imagined memory of the "primal scene" of the birth of Hebrew speech has disturbing similarities to the Freudian construction of the primal scene, although in the case of Ben-Avi, the child's perception of the father's aggressive behavior toward his wife is anything but a misunderstanding. Itamar Ben-Avi, by linking his first Hebrew words with both the rage of his father and the linguistic transgression of his mother, underlined the centrality of a parental and gender struggle in his own linguistic development. If we take all these accounts, including Ben-Yehuda's idealized one, as a collective myth of the Hebrew revival, it seems clear that the mother's silence, self-sacrifice, and absence (or, alternatively, her transgression) are built into the mythical structure.

I am not, it should be noted, arguing against the sincerity of Ben-Yehuda's perceived need for such radical measures as the linguistic quarantine of the first Hebrew-speaking child from his mother, the midwife, or a servant girl. But neither do I think that the silence, or silencing, of these women during the primal scene of the birth of modern Hebrew speech is trivial, secondary, or accidental, whether one reads the scenes I outlined above as literal truth or as myth. Given the educational patterns of Hebrew-Yiddish acquisition, there is a certain logic to Ben-Yehuda's changing the historical trajectory of the linguistic development of a Jewish child by prohibiting the speech of the child's mother. Moreover, Ben-Yehuda attempted to raise a child to speak Hebrew within the confines of the traditional Jewish family and in the larger setting of the old yishuv, with its conservative religious and social mores. The Hebrew revival finally succeeded under very different social and family circumstances, and its primary setting was not the home but the settlement school or its urban counterpart. In raising a Hebrew speaker within a traditional domestic Jewish environment, Ben-Yehuda may have had no choice but to substitute the paternal for the maternal role in the child's development.

Although Ben-Yehuda's experiment took place in an environment manifestly different from the ones in which the Hebrew revival eventually took hold, Ben-Yehuda became the symbol of the revival primarily during this later period. While it is not surprising that the proponents of the Hebrew revival would choose a hero from an earlier period, I argue that the narratives of Ben-Yehuda's life and vision served a particular purpose for later Hebraists. For one thing, Ben-Yehuda's domestic difficulties may well have proved the importance of combining a domestic and social revolution with the linguistic one.

But Ben-Yehuda's experience also encoded some of the larger difficulties inherent in the Hebrew revival, which was, on one level, the struggle between a "mother tongue" and a "father tongue." The revival of Hebrew as the living language of an entire population and the concomitant suppression of other languages (primarily Yiddish) that was so central to this project were accomplished without the aid of any state apparatus such as the one that succeeded in destroying the Soviet Hebrew literary scene. Instead, the revival of spoken Hebrew called into service an array of deeply rooted Jewish desires, prejudices, and anxieties, including, I will argue, psychosexual ones. The first attempts at Hebrew speech, as we have seen, both involved the Jewish woman in a more central role than other nationalist projects and reduced that role to its biological minimum. The Hebrew revival also implicated Jewish women because it commonly (though not universally) saw its task as the suppression of the Yiddish language, with its feminine associations. The growing Hebrew-speaking culture derived a sort of psychic momentum from actively stigmatizing what it saw as the womanly tongue and distancing itself from it. The revival operated in part according to what could be called a "politics of revulsion"; the Yiddish critic Avrom Golomb once argued that the Hebrew revival was motivated more strongly by hatred of Yiddish than by love for Hebrew.[17] Even if we take into account Golomb's Yiddishist bitterness, it seems clear that Hebrew was revived at least partially by tapping into a strong distaste for the disempowered diaspora existence that was often consciously or unconsciously perceived as having emasculated or feminized the Jewish collective; this distaste reflected itself, above all, in the rejection of the mame-loshn that both expressed and was the product of the objectionable Eastern European past.

Domestic strife around the issue of Hebrew speech continued for many years after the Hebrew revival was well under way. In a 1928 pamphlet, "The Hebrew Tongue on Women's Lips," Itamar Ben-Avi reported on the importance and difficulties of including women in the project of reviving Hebrew.

It seemed as if there was no hope that women in the holy city would utter Hebrew words. Even our great and beloved poet Yehuda Halevi, in spite of the beauty and softness of his verses, even he cannot give us the scent of the perfume that emanates from every word of our ancient rhetoricians. And do you know the reason for this? Because he never heard the music of the words of his tongue uttered by the lips of his mother, the lips of a woman, in his childhood. It is precisely this that is lacking in our language—womanhood! childhood![18]

In fact, women did increasingly contribute, in their role as mothers, writers, agricultural workers, and teachers, to the linguistic transformation of the yishuv.[19] Women like Nechama Feinstein-Pukhachevski, a writer who corresponded with Y. L. Gordon in Hebrew in the 1880s and raised a Hebrew-speaking child in Rishon-letsiyon in the 1890s, and Chemda Ben-Yehuda, who worked as a journalist and agitated for women's rights,[20] saw Hebraism and the struggle for women's equality as complementary causes. As early as 1889, Feinstein-Pukhachevski campaigned for Jewish women's education in Hebrew, albeit with the explicit goal of raising a new generation of children as Hebrew speakers.

It will do no good to worry about your sons' education, as long as you don't pay attention to the education of your daughters . . . to inscribe in their hearts love for their people and their brothers, so that they may bestow their holy spirit onto the generation that will be born onto their laps and make them loyal sons of their people.[21]

Feinstein-Pukhachevski and other women were welcomed into the circle of Hebrew speakers with a special warmth, since a Hebrew-speaking woman, as much as a Hebrew-speaking child, clearly signaled the dimensions of the Hebrew-language revolution and heralded its successful future. For Eliezer Ben-Yehuda, the contribution of women to the Hebrew revival was a necessary and valuable part of the national project and not just in their biological or educational roles.

The necessity of the hour is that the woman must penetrate Hebrew literature; only she can bring warmth, softness, flexibility, subtle, delicate, and shifting hues into the dead, forgotten, old, dry and hard Hebrew language. Simplicity and exactitude in the place of unbounded ornateness [*melitsah*, the flowery Hebrew style replete with biblical allusions characteristic of Haskalah writing].[22]

Ben-Yehuda was right to see women as the potential vehicles of a Hebrew style free of habitual allusion, one of the benefits of having remained outside the Hebrew textual system. Jewish women's historical exclusion from traditional Hebrew education became, in the first decades of the Hebrew revival, something of a blessing in disguise, since it enabled women writers to introduce not so much the "warmth" Ben-Yehuda sought as a flexible idiom free from the "echo chamber" of the traditional Hebrew library.[23] Rachel Katznelson-Shazar explicitly described the power of the poetry of Rachel, the Hebrew modernist, in these terms:

The literature of her time (Lamdan, Uri-Tsvi Greenberg, etc.) begins with the biblical verse, the sentence. With her it is the word. A word—an autonomous universe—with its literal content and sound. The word arose from the depths. Hatred and love, jealousy and forgiveness, appeasement and revenge, heights and depths understandable to everyone. How did her word acquire such weight? Because she learned it from the sources, with no commentaries, and because she was the one and only poet with her world, the world of a woman, which had no precedent in Hebrew poetry.[24]

The "sources," in Katznelson-Shazar's use of the word, are no longer the exalted texts of the Hebrew library but the more primary sources of individual expression "understandable to everyone." It was only in the modernist reevaluation of poetic style, that women's approach to Hebrew, "with no commentaries," could finally be perceived as a virtue.

Nevertheless, the road to full female participation in the Hebrew revival was a difficult one, given the head start a grounding in Jewish texts provided nascent Hebrew speakers. In 1929, the revisionist Zionist leader Zev Jabotinsky confirmed the impression that dedication to Hebrew in the yishuv sometimes bypassed the women: "Even the most fervent Zionist cannot guarantee that his wife is also a Zionist or that she takes his side with regard to the importance of Hebrew speech."[25] He may have been making rueful reference to his own situation. Y. Avineri related that Jabotinsky had to exempt his wife from the fines exacted by the "strict Hebrew police" enforcing Hebrew speech in their house because of the drain on his household finances (the "fine" was a small donation to a Zionist cause).[26] Although Zionists continually stressed the necessity of female participation in the Hebrew revival, it was clear to them that women were the segment of the population least able to make the transition to Hebrew speech quickly. Sometimes official concessions, mirroring Jabotinsky's private one, were made: in the 1930s, the Histadrut, the Zionist-Socialist Federation of Labor Unions, required Hebrew speech of all members, with the exception of "women who had been in the country for fewer than two years."[27] The labor organizers were not being chivalrous. They were operating on the assumption that even the most recent male immigrant could put together a Hebrew sentence from remembered fragments of a yeshiva or cheder education. No such assumption could be made for women.

A language revival with such built-in gender discrepancies could not fail to have profound cultural repercussions. The folklorist Alter Druyanov relates a riddle that circulated during the early years of the Hebrew revival: "Someone said that Erets-Israeli women are better than all other women in the world, since all other women talk without understanding, while the Erets-Israeli woman understands but does not speak."[28] In a note at the bottom of the page, Druyanov adds that the joke refers to women's difficulty in learning to speak Hebrew. The joke, if it was ever funny, derives a certain sadistic/comic power from more than just the difficulties women were having in mastering a language for which their education did not prepare them; it also invokes the stereotypical views of women as foolishly garrulous, "talk[ing] without understanding." Enforcing the language laws, as Ben-Yehuda was not the last husband to attempt to do, had the added "benefit" of finally silencing the talkative Jewish woman. And the quasi-talmudic form of the joke only reinforces the equation between men and proper Hebrew speech.

Even the debate over the proper pronunciation of Hebrew had sexual overtones. Ben-Yehuda characterized the Ashkenazic accentual system as "soft, weak, without the special strength the emphatic consonant gives to the word."[29] The preference for the Sephardic or Oriental accentual system was often described as a rejection of a weak and "whining" intonational pattern for a forceful accent as far removed from the Yiddish-inflected Hebrew as possible. Harshav has summarized the prevailing attitudes toward the two systems: "This is the perspective: our language is pioneering, coarse, strong, masculine—like the 'masculine' rhyme imposed by the Sephardi accent as opposed to the soft, 'feminine' rhyme dominant in Ashkenazi poetry (as in Italian)."[30] Jabotinsky pushed the accentual question further, campaigning for a Hebrew devoid of Yiddishisms and Eastern European "ghetto" intonations. In a letter to Dr. Yevin, the well-known Hebrew teacher, he describes his disgust on hearing Jewish women trying to speak Hebrew: "The woman says, 'Thank God, I'm much better,' but she speaks in a whining, almost sobbing tone, as if she were relating some disaster."[31] Jabotinsky's misogynist revulsion far exceeds the linguistic character of his observation: Hebrew intonation must distance itself from an entire mind-set, marked here as "feminine," that fuses complaint with euphemism (a typical Eastern European Yiddish speech act). What Jabotinsky insists on is not just a different accent or intonation but also a new type of speech performance, the straight-talking, clipped mode of address that has become increasingly identified with Israeli speech.[32] The revival, then, reinforced and solidified Hebrew's masculine associations in its adoption of particular speech patterns as well as a regnant Hebrew accent.

Ben-Yehuda's bookishness, his bourgeois image, his stubborn insistence on making the conservative city of Jerusalem the center of his pioneering linguistic efforts did not endear him to either his Orthodox neighbors or the later generations of Hebrew activists. Nevertheless, Ben-Yehuda's story acquired considerable cultural currency, and it continues to fascinate generations of Israelis. There are many reasons why this should be so, but among these I propose this one: for both Ben-Yehuda and the language pioneers that came later, Hebrew was not just a language, it was also a reorganization of traditional family structures and a recovery program for wounded Jewish masculinity.

II

Successive waves of immigration ensured that the work of Hebraist activists remained necessary. Nevertheless, victories began to mount. While the first revivers of spoken Hebrew told stories about the thin veneer of Hebrew speech breaking under the impact of fever or in a husband's absence, later generations of Zionists increasingly had wondrous tales to recount, especially of the children who had been born and educated in the new Hebrew schools of the yishuv. Anecdotal material about the new generation of Hebrew-speaking children reveals how profoundly the linguistic transformation symbolized a psychosexual one. Whereas the Ben-Yehuda family drama had pitted male against female speech, the new psycholinguistic drama was taking place within the structure of Jewish masculinity. Itamar Even-Zohar, with barely concealed pride in the macho character of Hebrew, in the success of Zionism at "transforming the identity, the very nature of the people," relates the well-known story of the visit of two Yiddishists to pre–World War I Tel Aviv who watch the schoolboys leave the Herzliya Gymnasium after classes have been dismissed for the day.

The elder one says to the other: "The Zionists boast that Hebrew is becoming the natural tongue for the children of Palestine. I will show you that they are lying. I will tweak one of the boy's ears, and I promise you that he will not cry out 'Ima' but 'mame' in Yiddish."
    So saying, he approached one of the boys and tweaked his ear. The boy turned on him and shouted "hamor" [donkey, in Hebrew]. The Yiddishist turned to his friend and said: "I'm afraid the Zionists are right."[33]

This anecdote is so similar to others that arose about different figures (usually connected in some way with Yiddish) that one can detect in it a "joke type." The success stories of the Hebrew revival, and this anecdote is of course an example, often involved children, as in the Yiddish poet Yehoash's awed report of the Tel Aviv street urchins playing ball "in Hebrew."[34] The awe of older Yiddish-speaking Jews visiting Palestine, either sincere or exaggerated by proud Hebraists, seems to apply equally to the two—presumably related—phenomena: children speaking Hebrew and *Jewish* children playing ball. The implications of the anecdote about the two Yiddishists, however, go further than the suggestion that the new generation has succeeded in acquiring a new mother tongue or even that it enjoys sports. Itamar Even-Zohar interprets this joke as suggesting that "a nation cannot be tweaked by the ear and cry 'mother,' that is, run for help to its mother. The 'Jewish mother' thus had become culturally incomprehensible."[35] Implicit in all the anecdotes related here is not only the obsolescence of the "Jewish mother" but also the replacement of the despised diaspora "femininity" with a new model for Jewish masculine behavior. Mame-loshn is, literally, the language of "mama's boys," whereas Hebrew is the language of the ferocious, disrespectful young.

Yeshurun Keshet relates another anecdote that circulated somewhat later, after the refugees of Hitler's Europe began to arrive: a refugee child in one of the temporary camps that had been set up beside a kibbutz ran crying home to his mother, "Mame, di hebre'ishe shkotsim'lekh viln mikh shlogn" (Mama, the little Hebrew gentile boys want to hit me).[36] Keshet's story captures the difference between the Yiddish-speaking diasporic Jewish male, clinging to his mother in fear and helplessness, and his fierce Hebrew counterpart, who is associated, in the mind of the Yiddish child, with the non-Jewish hoodlums of Europe. The new Hebrew male, this anecdote seems to be saying, is so different from his diasporic other that recognizing him as Jewish requires a major shift in the Jewish/non-Jewish paradigm. This last story, however, has a pathos lacking in the jokes I related earlier, since the young refugee boy is genuinely afraid, unlike the older Yiddishists. The unadulterated pride with which the earlier anecdotes were repeated is somewhat mixed, in this anecdote, with the bittersweet regret that overtook even the most fervent Hebraists in the wake of the genocide of European Jewry.

It is no coincidence, perhaps, that one of the most notorious acts of hostility by the militant Brigade for the Defense of the Language was its struggle in the autumn of 1930 against the showing of the Yiddish film Di yidishe mame, which Arye Pilovski describes as of "extremely limited aesthetic value" but which was nevertheless the occasion of an international Jewish scandal.[37] Pilovski relates that the film was only shown after protests and threats under the protection of the British police, and even then the brigade succeeded in disrupting the event. When additional screenings were canceled, the Yiddish press decried the "pogrom" against Yiddish in Palestine.[38] Yosef Klausner, in an article protesting the film when it was first scheduled, explained the Hebraist fervor as implicitly connected with the film, rather than merely finding a convenient scapegoat in it. As Klausner put it, Yiddish was dangerous precisely because it was the language of "our mothers and the masses."[39] The sentimental Yiddish film, with its clear call for loyalty to the Jewish mother and its appeal to a broad audience, represented more than just a linguistic danger to new Hebrew speakers. It also threatened to wear down the emotional barriers that the Hebrew pioneers shored up not only against Yiddish but also against its symbolic attractions.

At least some of what is at stake in these stories transcends the Hebrew revival and the Hebrew-Yiddish conflict. The Zionist embrace of masculinism has derivations other than the Hebrew-Yiddish language conflict. The fin-de-siècle Central European cult of youth and athletics (and in a previous generation, dueling fraternities) certainly contributed to Zionist culture. Theodor Herzl envisioned Zionism as a means by which Jews could "become real men." Michael Berkowitz describes the Zionist agenda as follows:

> [Herzl's] attitude, shared by most early Zionists, was an internal and external disavowal of the anti-Semitic stereotype of Jewish men as unmanly, and it affirmed the European-wide equation of manliness and rightful membership in the nation. The way to a "new Jewish existence" could only be reached through participation in a "society of friends," or "a special type of comradeship" that was possible for Jewish men only through Zionism. This myth reflected the reality of a movement, which, like the larger society, was male-dominated. The inaugural assembly of 250 Zionists included only around twelve female delegates, and women were not accorded voting rights until the Second Congress. To be a Zionist was to "take a manly stand" and be a manly man, asserting the Jews' rightful place among the people of the world.[40]

Max Nordau's influential speech on "Muskeljudentum" (Jewry of Muscle) on the opening of the Zionist sports organization Bar Kokhba is perhaps the clearest statement of the necessity of improving the physical prowess of feminized Jewish men. In a passionate appeal for global Jewish transformation, Nordau contrasts the stereotypical Jewish male with his vision for a new variety of Jewish masculinity, but one that was once the rightful property of Jewish men: "In the narrow Jewish street our poor limbs soon forgot their gay movements; in the dimness of sunless houses our eyes began to blink shyly. . . . Let us take up our oldest traditions; let us once more become deep-chested, sturdy, sharp-eyed men."[41]

Considering the degree to which Hebraism was intended as a program for the most fundamental self-transformation, it is not surprising that the first step in Hebraization often entailed a name change, or that the Brigade considered it a public service to help people Hebraize their names. Elon describes the practice of name changing (which appears in a number of biblical stories) as a "magical" act. The Hebraizing of diaspora names can be traced to

the old Jewish custom of changing the name of a very sick man in the hope of cheating the angel of death. Thus, it may be more than accident that so many Jewish refugees from lands of persecution—even more often their sons—have shown a proclivity to redefine themselves with names that denote firmness, toughness, strength, courage, and vigor: *Yariv* ("antagonist"); *Oz* ("strength"); *Tamir* ("towering"); *Lahat* ("blaze"); *Kabiri* ("tremendous"); *Hod* ("splendor," "majesty"); *Barak* ("lightning"); *Tsur* ("rock"); *Nechushtan* ("bronze"); *Bar Adon* ("son of the master," or "masterful"); or even *Bar Shilton* ("fit to govern").[42]

Although the Hebraization of women's family names typically followed that of their husbands or fathers, sometimes women took the opportunity of the widespread name changes to take on their own Hebrew names; these names can reveal something to us about how self-transformation was viewed by women, who could be assumed to be outside the cult of Hebraic masculinism. Among the most prominent examples are writers like Rachel, who dropped her family name altogether. Rachel's use of her first name alone, which is in keeping with her poetics of simplicity, might also signal a newfound freedom from both the European past and her own family history. The name also serves to present the poet as a neobiblical character or as a woman with whom her reading public could feel itself on an intimate first-name basis. The Hebrew poet Yocheved Bat-Miriam (the daughter of Miriam) chose a matronym, as Ilana Pardes calls it, thus adopting her own foremother as a voluntary family affiliation. "Bat-Miriam's choice of a name," Pardes argues, "needs to be seen both as a concrete challenge to the patrilinear naming system and as a critique of culture in which literary tradition, like names, is passed down from father to son."[43]

In feminine reworkings of Zionist/Hebraist practice such as Bat-Miriam's, the desire to forge a connection with the biblical past often turned out to contain an element of feminist subversion (just as the feminine use of the biblical topos "land = beloved woman" could produce a lesbian rather than a normative heterosexual love poem). In the case of Bat-Miriam's adoption of a name, the reversal of a biblical parent-child relationship—in the Bible Yocheved is the mother of Miriam—in the modern Hebrew name can also be seen in the light of the Zionist reversal of the parent-child hierarchy. Here, the biblical mother becomes the daughter's daughter, or alternatively, the biblical daughter becomes the mother's mother, so that biological affiliation and the respect and authority traditionally invested in the older generation give way to a fluid model of imaginative and voluntary affiliations.

Other women writers chose names from nature, as did many men. Malka Shechtman, for instance, called herself Bat-Chama, daughter of the sun.[44] Again, in cases like these, the feminine version of the Zionist model often contained an additional revolutionary element, since the women were clearly setting up a personal rather than a dynastic or family model of name transmission. A brief perusal of a collection of articles by Zionist women workers published in 1930 suggests how widespread such name changes were among women: of forty-five contributors, ten used only their first names and three used a single initial as a surname. Among these ten, two names are of Yiddish origin while one is European; the others are Hebrew names (it is impossible to decide whether these names were adopted, though names like Carmela and Techiya have a distinctly Zionist ring). Of the family names, one, Bat-Rachel, is a matronym. One woman signs herself Dinah Bat-Chorin (Dinah the Free Woman, or Dinah the Daughter of a Free Person), while another one is called Nechama Bat-Tsiyon (Nechama the Daughter of Zion).[45] A woman taking a name like Bat-Chorin or Bat-Tsiyon was doing more than transforming a Yiddish family name into a Hebrew one; she was also rejecting the patriarchal transmission of family names. To adopt a family name with a clear feminine marker, even as a pen name, was to declare independence from husband and father.

In other cases, name changes revealed both the revolutionary discontinuities called for by Hebraism and the submerged continuities that managed to survive even the most extreme attempts at Zionist self-transformation. The Hebrew poet Avot Yeshurun, in an interview in the mid-1970s, explained how and why he changed his name from Yechiel Perlmutter. The name change was not only from a diasporic name to a Hebrew one but also from a name with a recognizable Yiddish meaning (Pearl-mother, or Mother-of-Pearl), which includes a reference to "mother" rare in a family name, to a Hebrew name that means either "fathers of Jerusalem" or "Fathers are watching us" (Avot, fathers; Yeshurun, "are or will be watching us"). When the interviewer asked Yeshurun about his unusual name, the poet answered that he had chosen the first name, Avot, on his first day in the army, immediately after the founding of the state of Israel. He had long wanted to change his name, but he felt particularly strongly that he should have a Hebrew name for the swearing-in ceremony that was to take place the following day. Yeshurun described how he had lain awake most of the night, trying to think of a name that would suit him.

At dawn, I said to myself: remember your childhood. Maybe I could come up with something from my childhood. I remembered my mother singing beautiful lullabies to my brothers in her beautiful voice. Once, she bent over the cradle and sang to the youngest one in Yiddish and Ukrainian. But the children wouldn't fall asleep, and my mother stopped singing and instead called out excitedly, "*tatelekh, tatelekh*" [a common Yiddish endearment meaning "little fathers, little fathers"]. And then the child understood that she wasn't going to sing and he went to sleep himself. From this I took the name "Avot" and was very satisfied with it.[46]

Yeshurun's story is emblematic in a number of ways. The first of these might be the poet's sense of the importance of finding himself a Hebrew name for the occasion of his induction into the new Israeli army. Any Hebrew name would signify a new masculinity, given the associations of the language with the proud biblical history of Jewish sovereignty; but Yeshurun was not simply translating his name from German or Russian into Hebrew, as many did, but selecting a name that would confer a new identity befitting a Hebrew warrior. In calling himself Avot, he not only chose a name that would signify his belief in a new and powerful connection with his patrilineage, he also erased the old name, with its associations of femininity and its recognizably Yiddish sound. If we read Avot as a replacement of his previous first name Yechiel (God lives or will live), another theme becomes prominent. In this substitution, the modern Hebrew name presents a human—albeit male—history in the place of the traditional Hebrew (or Yiddishized) Jewish name that refers to divine faith. Instead of asserting the existence and authority of God, the new name asserts the human continuities of Jewish history.

Nevertheless, the account Yeshurun gives of his self-transformation also indicates that his name expressed a strong sense of continuity with his past, in the form of his Yiddish-speaking mother. The name Avot, for all its patriarchal grandeur, in fact is a translation of the Yiddish term used for little boys, "little fathers." Translated back into Yiddish, the name means "little boys are watching us," as if Yeshurun were reversing the course of his own history or imagining his present circumstances from the amazed perspective of a little Eastern European child. The disappearance of the diminutive in the move to Hebrew might signal the process of replacing a Yiddish childhood with a Hebrew adulthood, but it might also be a clever concealment of the continuing existence of the Yiddish boy. Yeshurun's memorializing of his mother is also curiously ambiguous. By having her choose his name, as it were, he admits her continued importance to his new life. But the story of his choice and the name itself also signify her absence, erasure, or silence. The name comes, that is, at the moment when the mother breaks off her lullaby and moves away, just as the young man chose his name at the moment when his youth would be ruptured by his shouldering of the adult burdens of a Zionist soldier. This account, in all its complexity, reveals something of the ways in which radical discontinuity and continuity combine with masculine/feminine models of identity in the Zionist narrative.

III

The discussion of Hebrew and Yiddish occurred not at the margins of the Yiddishist canon but at its very center. Major Yiddish writers dedicated many poems to the struggle for the survival of Yiddish and against Hebraist claims. To read the outlines of the Hebrew-Yiddish language war in the Hebraist environment, however, requires an attention to the sub-canonical and marginal texts of the period. The Hebrew writers of the *moderna* (the Hebrew modernist generation) perceived their greatest achievement as the creation of a monolingual, "natural" Hebrew, one that could express their new environment without undue self-consciousness or linguistic borrowing. But the margins of this literature attest to the strain of defending the borders of this monolingualism and reveal the traces of what was suppressed in the creation of modern and of modernist Hebrew literature. Yiddish literature, by way of contrast, could afford to address directly the Hebrew it could also easily encompass in its own linguistic repertoire.

Yiddishists confronted with the sexual politics of the Hebrew-Yiddish language war had two choices. They could resist the identification of Yiddish with women and insist on its status as the language of the "masses"; Yehoash's new Yiddish translation of the Bible would certainly be counted among the efforts to reenvision Yiddish as a language for men as well as women. Or they could emphasize Yiddish's feminine roots. The Yiddish writer Y. L. Peretz's speech at the 1908 Tshernovits Yiddish Conference provided modern Yiddish literature with both its patrilineage and its matrilineage. Peretz's genealogy implies the continuity between the older Yiddish literature for women and the newer Yiddish literature, which also responds to the needs of a marginalized public.

Yiddish literature does not begin with Isaac Meir Dik. Its "Genesis" is the Chasidic tale. . . . But then the Jewish woman, the young Jewish girl also demanded something for herself. With that we get the "books for women." And *ivre-teytsh* became *mame-loshn*.

The Jewish people have two languages. The first one is for the studious men in the study hall: the language of Torah, of Talmud; and the second one for the masses, and for the Jewish daughter. . . . And then comes the Jewish worker, who finds his tools for survival, for a workers' culture, in Yiddish.[47]

The Yiddish novelist Sholem Ash, also speaking at the conference, presented a resolution to translate the Bible into Yiddish (a project ultimately realized by the poet Yehoash). Ash both acknowledged the need for a more modern translation than the *Tsenerene*, which was not, strictly speaking, a translation at all, and paid tribute to the women's literature that "preserved our folk-spirit . . . and from [which] we have been spiritually nourished."[48]

Debates about the status of Yiddish circled and recircled the territory Peretz and Ash laid out in Tshernovits with surprising tenacity. The project of translating the Bible into Yiddish suggested that Yiddish now had to serve the needs of a new audience, one defined by class or ideological interests rather than gender. The translation of the Bible into Yiddish, it was felt, would set Yiddish on the level of other world languages, on the one hand, and of Hebrew, on the other. As Katznelson-Shazar described what she saw as the illogical argument for the translation: "Can the Hebrew Bible be translated into all languages and not Yiddish, the language of the Jews, so that those Jews who know only Yiddish won't know the Bible?"[49] For her, this rhetorical question was illogical precisely because it saw an equivalence between Yiddish and other languages.

You can translate the Bible into German or English, because there is an equality between those languages and the language of the Bible, an equality that does not exist between that language and Yiddish; because no two languages have such different programs as those two, because we divided the contents of our lives between them.[50]

In these remarks, Katznelson-Shazar lays out the perception many Yiddishists were combatting, that Yiddish would always be a partial language, doomed to a complementary and subsidiary role in relation to Hebrew. Set in these terms, it becomes clear why a new translation of the Bible should have been perceived as so (paradoxically) necessary for demonstrating Yiddish's independence from Hebrew.

While many Yiddishists preferred to set the female audience for Yiddish literature in the past, staking out new territory for the language, others celebrated precisely this feminine history. The major Yiddish poet Yankev Glatshteyn, who published his first poems under a female pseudonym, made the most of the connections between Yiddish and women, often taking the part of women and Yiddish simultaneously. In his 1929 collection *Kredos*, Glatshteyn responds to the ill treatment of the Yiddish writers in the yishuv in poems that often embody the silenced other of these poems in female characters. One poem is entitled "There Where the Cedars," in an ironic reference to the well-known song "There Where the Cedars Bloom" sung by German-speaking Zionists, which is itself reworked from a patriotic German song, "The Watch on the Rhine," popular at the turn of the century. The German original is evident behind the revised Zionist lyrics:

> There where the cedar kisses the sky,
> And where the Jordan quickly flows by,
> There where the ashes of my father lie,
> In that exalted Reich, on sea and sand,
> Is my beloved, true Fatherland.[51]

While the father and "Fatherland" are prominent in the Zionist version of the song, Glatshteyn's portrait of "where the cedars bloom" (the title cannot be bothered to complete the trite phrase) foregrounds the women who have been omitted in the other version, replacing "the ashes of my father" with the living, if silent, matriarch Rachel:

> There where the cedars bloom—
> They don't let you speak Yiddish.
> They don't let my language touch the lips.
> Mother Rachel, who cried her way through the entire
>   *taytsh-chumesh*,
> Lies at the crossroad and waits, silent—
> She would cry for her children
> But she only knows Zhargon.[52]

The power of Glatshteyn's Yiddishist message lies not only in its sentimental rhetoric of maternity but also in its appropriation of Zionist themes, beginning with the title (and Glatshteyn, later in the poem, uses some Hebrew as well) and continuing with the claim that the matriarch Rachel properly belongs, not to the Hebrew Bible or to the Holy Land, but to the Yiddish translation of the Bible for women and to her diaspora children. Glatshteyn's ploy could work, of course, not only because Rachel has been associated with the diaspora but also because of the associations he could count on his audience to make between Yiddish and women, especially older women.

Glatshteyn's bitterness at the Zionist suppression of Yiddish long outlasted the years of the outright "language war." In a poem first published in 1961, "Ret tsu mir yidish" (Speak Yiddish with Me), the poetic speaker calls Israel "my Yiddish (or Jewish) country" and promises to answer in Hebrew if he is addressed in Yiddish. In the earlier poem, Glatshteyn used the figure of Rachel to personify the silenced language. Here, however, it is the men who suffer the brunt of the repression, while the women are still allowed some leeway in their expressive freedom. Thus the poetic speaker discovers a loophole in the masculinist Hebrew program, finding a conversational partner in the Jewish woman. The different status of men and women in the Hebrew project is implied in the second stanza, where he spies his "grandparents," the patriarchs Abraham and Sarah (of course, Yankev is the Yiddish form of Jacob, the grandson of Abraham and Sarah):

> God help us, Grandpa-Grandma.
> Abraham is crossing the street in silence.
> Don't take it to heart, Yankele,
> Says Sarah, he understands every word.
>
> That's the way it goes here.
> A man has to stifle his Yiddish.
> But a Jewess from the *yidish-taytsh*
> Still has something to say.

Sarah comforts Yankele, the poetic persona, by reassuring him that although Avrom is silent, "Hu meyvin kol dibur" (He understands every word)—a Hebrew code phrase inserted into Yiddish speech to warn the interlocutor that a nearby non-Jew can understand Yiddish, as Janet Hadda points out in her analysis of this poem.[53] Thus the poem enacts two dislocations of traditional Jewish values, one social and one linguistic: the patriarchs are imagined as Yiddish speakers, as generations of Ashkenazic domestications of biblical figures had rendered them; and as Yiddish speakers, they are treated as outsiders in the Jewish state. In this context, the function of the Hebrew code phrase is completely reversed, working to reassure Yankele that Abraham is not an outsider rather than warning him that he is. Glatshteyn's clever reminders of the historical interconnectedness of Hebrew and Yiddish reinforce the poem's message that Hebrew speakers may not have changed as completely as the Zionists boast.

The discourse of linguistic maternity was so powerful that Hebraists could not completely cede the role of "mother tongue" to Yiddish. Arguing for the sole legitimacy of Hebrew as the Jewish national tongue, Achad Ha'am rhetorically asked whether the proper language for an individual can be any but the one in which "they sang to him lullabies, that was rooted in his soul before he even knew who he was and which developed along with him."[54] What is true for the individual, Achad Ha'am claims, is also true for the nation. But the rhetorical move he makes in this passage is a contradictory one, since the metaphorical mother tongue of his audience (as a national collective) may have been Hebrew but the one in which many of them were in fact lulled to sleep was Yiddish. At stake, of course, was not only the emotional power of this maternal rhetoric but also the long-entrenched connections between nationality and the concept of mother tongue. Thus Achad Ha'am needed to establish a matrilineal heritage for Hebrew, not only the readily available patrilineal one. While thirty years before, only those writers who chose Yiddish were expected to defend their language choice, now the Yiddishists had a "natural" claim to their language that Hebrew ideologues were at pains to duplicate.

IV

In 1927, the Yiddish writers Sholem Ash and Perets Hirshbein visited Palestine to witness the Zionist revolution and make a gesture of goodwill and reconciliation with the Hebraists. Over the objections of some of the younger and more militantly Hebraist of its members, the Hebrew Writers Union arranged a reception in their honor. The Hebrew poet Chayim Nachman Bialik gave the keynote address, sounding the familiar note of Hebrew-Yiddish complementarity to welcome the Yiddish writers but subtly reminding the audience, as well, of the hierarchy that governed the relationship between Hebrew and Yiddish. Bialik began his speech by alluding to the hostility with which he had been received in New York a few years before and noting the warm welcome extended to the Yiddish writers in Tel Aviv, since, "thank God," the Hebrew-Yiddish language war had already been settled in Palestine. A newspaper report the following day summarized the rest of his speech.

Hebrew and Yiddish are a marriage made in heaven that can never be sundered, just like Ruth and Naomi, but the very instant that Yiddish tries to cut herself off from Hebrew, she ceases to be ours. . . . The edict of Rabbenu Gershom [against bigamy] does not apply to languages at the present.[55]

Bialik begins by describing Hebrew-Yiddish relations through the presumably necessary institution of marriage, a fated and irrevocable link. In the next phrase, though, Hebrew and Yiddish are tied by something closer to a friendship between women. This partnership, moreover, is between a Jewish woman and one whose origins are non-Jewish (presumably like Yiddish). Yiddish, like Ruth, is a visitor in Palestine on sufferance and liable to be evicted if she does not follow the rules and stick close to Naomi. The transformation of the married couple into a pair of women apparently called to Bialik's mind that other familiar trope the Yiddish cartoonists loved to exploit: the writer "at the present" may, if he chooses, take two wives. The language laws are more permissive, in this analogy, than those that govern Jewish marriages.

Over the next few days, the Socialist-Zionist organ of the Hebrew Writers Union recorded the reactions of other Hebrew writers to the polite welcome accorded the visiting emissaries from the world of Yiddish. The writers who boycotted the reception were primarily of a younger generation, and their responses had nothing of the tempered good manners the speeches at the reception had demonstrated. The younger Hebrew poet Avraham Shlonsky described the reception as a farce, an empty diplomatic ceremony that could not mask the urgent need for a decisive stance on the language question. In a direct and disdainful reference to Bialik's moderate position on Yiddish in Palestine, Shlonsky attacked those who signed the "marriage contract" without acquiring the power of attorney from the Hebrew camp.

We never accepted the match between the languages, so we're not going to dance at the wedding. And we're not going to wait for any Rabbenu Gershom to make a rabbinical decree against multilingualism. . . . We want our Erets-Israeli breath to be purely Hebrew. With both lungs![56]

Shlonsky's response to Bialik's pious blessing of the eternal linguistic union of Hebrew and Yiddish became a rallying cry, but not because it shed any new light on the language question: after all, Shlonsky did no more than rephrase Bialik's remarks in the negative. Shlonsky's slogan, "We never accepted the match between the languages," was echoed because he succeeded in fusing a revolutionary sexual ethic with a call for an exclusive loyalty to Hebrew. Bialik projected the Hebraist disavowal of Yiddish onto the camp of the Yiddishists, claiming that Hebrew had no need to mistreat Yiddish and was in the position to make grand gestures of acceptance. By contrast, Shlonsky took full, conscious responsibility for the ideological repudiation of Yiddish, using this repudiation to launch a generational war against the poetic norms of Bialik and his epigones. And while Bialik's words are no more than a mildly clever extension of an exhausted metaphor, as automatic as the *melitsah* allusiveness Shlonsky decried in his futurist manifestos of the early twenties,

Shlonsky's answer recharges the metaphor's dormant sexual dimension. Shlonsky, as the fiery revolutionary of the *moderna*, had to counter the implication in Bialik's speech that openness to Yiddish was somehow connected with sexual freedom. He did so by announcing that his own disinterest in having two women had nothing to do with conformity to rabbinical law. In Shlonsky's formulation, the move to a revitalized Hebrew and away from Yiddish requires no apology or concession to tradition. Shlonsky takes Bialik's heterosexual metaphor and reworks it into a rejection of marital laws and a plea for the health of the solitary body who "breathes" Hebrew with both lungs (presumably rather than splitting his lung capacity between two languages). Hebraism, for Shlonsky, is a gesture of both literary and erotic freedom, an expression of (masculine) liberation from both a conservative literary code and a repressive sexual order.

Historians have begun to explore the degree to which the Zionist revolution was also an erotic revolution, to use David Biale's resonant phrase.[57] But it is also true that the rhetoric of Hebraism and Hebrew modernism—including the discourse of the Hebrew-Yiddish language war—was intricately connected with that of erotic transformation. The twenties, in particular, saw an explosion of manifestos, speeches, and poems that championed Hebrew modernism alongside with and as an expression of a new sexual ethos. Bialik's and Shlonsky's remarks on the status of Yiddish in Palestine made full use of what had become, by 1927, a ramified and condensed code for talking about the language conflict and the sexual promises of the Zionist experiment simultaneously.

Shlonsky's rhetorical stance in the Ash-Hirshbein affair, then, was part of a larger project of infusing the new Hebrew poetry with the energy and dynamism of a sexual (as well as political) revolution. For Shlonsky, the Russian Revolution, which he admired, demanded a reshaping of poetic style, a transformation he thought of as intimately connected with a new model of manhood. The poetry of his day was too feminine, too timid, false, and ornamental, Shlonsky argued in a 1923 manifesto.

Do you remember Pisagov? He wanted to hear a coquettish woman speak in a simple, natural voice. What did he do? He snuck up behind her back and with a block of wood—hit her on the head! And when a great shout came out of the startled and wounded woman, he knew: This is her natural voice!

That's it! There is too much of the feminine in literature and especially in poetry: it minces, acts charming, and flirts.

World literature should have been knocked on the head by the Russian Revolution, so that the natural voice of humanity should ring out, the voice of the poet, the voice of pain! Only in prison did the dandy Oscar Wilde begin to speak in a human voice, and the word "sorrow" first flowed from his pen in "De Profundis."[58]

What the pain and shock of revolution could do for literature, Shlonsky argues, was to rid poetry of the coquette and the dandy, the woman and the homosexual.

More usually, Shlonsky spoke of the poetic revolution of his generation in terms of a revolt against the sexual constraints of an earlier day. In a 1922 manifesto, Shlonsky made particularly brilliant use of the rhetoric of sexual revolution to describe modernist changes in Hebrew poetics; he compared the previous generation's sublime style of compulsory biblical allusions to a traditional marriage in which sexual relations have become habitual and automatic. The Hebrew modernist rejection of allusiveness, in Shlonsky's formulation, echoes the calls for free love and erotic liberation that characterized some aspects of the Zionist social experiment.

Civil marriage, free love between words, without arranged matches of style, without family pedigrees and dowries of associations, and most important: without the bridal canopy and the marital blessings! (There is too much family purity in our language!)
Any combination of words—lawless attachments, one-night stands.[59]

Zohar Shavit, in her study of yishuv literature and ideology, interprets Shlonsky's vehement attack on Bialik's stance toward Yiddish as merely a pretext for his poetic revolution against the hegemony of Bialik's style.[60] But in an important sense, the internal poetic struggles of Hebrew literature and the larger linguistic conflict intersected. By the twenties and thirties, with the growth of spoken Hebrew in Palestine, Hebrew was itself developing what could be called "internal diglossia," with the gap between the lofty quasi-biblical style that characterized the Hebrew poetry of Bialik's generation and the vernacular that could already be heard on the streets of Tel Aviv becoming increasingly apparent to the younger generation of writers. Thus Shlonsky's explicit agenda of lowering the register of Hebrew poetry, one he only partially realized, demanded a double-pronged attack—first, on the sublime style of Bialik and his epigones, and second, on the threatened encroachment (and historical primacy) of Yiddish as the modern Jewish vernacular. And he could use similar rhetorical strategies in both battles, since the Hebrew high style and the Yiddish vernacular were part of the same traditional structure that was encoded in and exemplified by rigid and stultifying gender codes. The Hebrew sublime and the denigrated Yiddish coarse speech, in other words, are two sides of the same obsolete coin. Shlonsky's radical refusal of bilingualism, and his couching of this refusal in a marital metaphor, recalls Ben-Yehuda's determination to create a "pure" Hebrew atmosphere for what Harshav refers to as the First Hebrew Child. Both projects combine the creation of a monolingual environment with the refusal of female company and feminine speech.

The poet Uri-Tsvi Greenberg stands at the other end of the ideological spectrum from Shlonsky, but their modernist programs are remarkably similar in linking Hebraism with a new masculinity. Greenberg began his literary career as a Yiddish poet, moving to Hebrew poetry and right-wing Zionism only after migrating to Palestine in 1923. His 1926 *Masculinity Rising* describes the poetic speaker's immigration to Palestine and subsequent shift to writing in Hebrew as a psychosexual transformation. The section "From the Depths" (or "De Profundis") combines the language of Psalms and the long, overheated phrases of expressionism to lament the poet's descent into the mires of European promiscuity and decadence. Whereas Wilde's sojourn in prison, as Shlonsky saw it, meant his abandonment of dandyism, Greenberg associates the depths with the degradation of an emasculating, hyperactive heterosexuality.

> (Meanwhile: a smartly pressed body, bowtie on the chest, fragrantly coiffed
>   hair, patent-leather shoes, a sneer, and a cigarette . . .) . . .
>
> And even he did not come to me: my savior—madness, to
>   rescue me from woman, from law, and from poesy—
>   from the prison of the phrase . . .
> And I, even then I was a Nazirite-of-sorrow: biting my lips when
>   nobody was watching, full of gangrene inside,
> Even when I gave a quivering body to the fornications of ten women—
> For I hated the woman with a pity as rigid as metal and the lie became
>   holy, because I pitied the corpse that the lie flung down beneath
>   me.[61]

The poem echoes Marinetti's famous futurist call for freedom from women, the past, and the well-ordered sentence; this poetic speaker, though, is still imprisoned in these bonds. There is hope for him: even in the embrace of the woman, "the corpse that the lie flung down beneath me," the poet retains the asceticism that will reach fruition in the rigors of pioneer life in Palestine.

In the next poem of the cycle, "In the Land of the Prophets," the suffering European poet is saved from his sexual and literary hell not by madness but by the Jerusalem air, the company of comrades, and the Hebrew language, which together produce a body-text punctuated by what could be called an electric masculinity.

> Exclamation points are shouted into my flesh like lightning bolts. Masculinity rising in the climate of the land of the prophets
> And I was born in Poland a soft child of Judaism and my father's oldest son
> (How could this Jerusalem body have been born in Poland?)[62]

Just as "From the Depths" sets the poet off from his decadent surroundings even as he participates most fully in its rituals, "In the Land of the Prophets" carries the memory—wondrous or anxious—of the "soft child" of the diaspora in the thrill of self-transformation. Greenberg's rhetorical question measures not only the distance traveled from his contingent, inappropriate birth but also the potential instability of the Zionist transformation of the male Jew.

In Greenberg's 1928 manifesto *To the Ninety Nine*, the effeminacy he rails against is no longer in the European past; in a scornful tirade against the vast majority of Hebrew writers, Greenberg dismisses Hebrew poetry as a literature of "manicured nails," a "spoiled queen in silk slippers."[63] Like Shlonsky, Greenberg believed that the new poetic style required an escape from the restraints of an old order that emasculated and domesticated the male poet. In the passage that most clearly connects domesticity and traditionalism with women, Greenberg slyly praises the instincts of the common man over those of the hidebound, sentimental, Hebrew poet.

The common man, when the storm has blown over, comes out of hiding and asks the Rabbi: "Is my wife permitted or forbidden me?" The common man understands that a catastrophe has occurred. The poet, though, when the rioters have passed, comes out of hiding and peeks: at the sun and the blooming acacia . . . and doesn't ask the exposed and hushed life about his muse, what is his muse to him now in this bloodstained world? She continues to be his beloved to the end of time.[64]

The allusion here, of course, is to Bialik's famous poem on the Kishinev pogrom "In the City of Slaughter." In Bialik's poem, though, it is the priests (who have a stricter marital code) who emerge from hiding to ask if they can resume relations with a wife who has been raped: "Rabbi, is my wife permitted or forbidden to me?" Bialik bitterly continues:

"And everything goes back to the way it was, everything is normal again." Greenberg audaciously reverses what is itself a searing indictment of Jewish political passivity. In his version, the man who questions whether he can resume relations with his wife is not servile and politically impotent but rather the only one who recognizes the power of historical trauma to disrupt domestic tranquility. By contrast, the Hebrew poet's return to his beloved muse attests to his blindness to the horrors of contemporary life. The proper response to the ravages of the present is a rejection of sentiment and convention, in literature as in nation building.

The sense that Hebrew liberated its speakers from an antiquated domestic order was sometimes expressed by women as well, although usually the fatal femininity was located in the older generation. Rachel Katznelson-Shazar, the critic and editor of the *Woman Workers' Word* who also moved from the Yiddish camp to Hebraism, described Hebrew as a revolutionary language, freeing its speakers from a stifling maternal embrace.

There was something in Yiddish literature that reminded one of a mother. Its writers couldn't see or artistically penetrate into the inner lives of our distressed people. In the same way, the mother cannot see in the soul of her son all his inner wars, his sins, for, after all, he is her son and she is just a mother. . . .

In those days, right after the [failed] 1905 Russian revolution, when our nation was under such stress, there was something soporific in the best of Yiddish literature, a lack of wings, and it was hard to breathe in its presence. There was a time when the shtetl was exactly the same for us as it was for [Sholem] Ash: a special world, self-sustaining and nourished from its own beauty, but that's not what we needed then, on the eve of the Second Aliya. For if all we had was the capacity to see and think as it was revealed in Yiddish, we could no longer have thought our people to be one of the great nations.[65]

Katznelson-Shazar contrasts the narrow horizons of Yiddish literature with the greater scope of Hebrew literature, which can see past the limited world of small-town Eastern Europe. Unlike her male counterparts, she continued to express the attractions of the mother tongue, even if they turn out to be ultimately illusory. For Katznelson-Shazar, it is the older generation of women who personify Yiddish, not her own—and this may be the move that allows her to participate so fervently in the sexually charged rhetoric of Hebraism. In this passage, she tells the story of rejecting the mother tongue not as the rejection of femininity per se but as the necessary break from the stifling maternal nest.

The poems and manifestos of international modernism express the conviction that the old ways of life, including the traditional sexual and domestic order, were exploding—or should be. For the Zionist modernist writers who left family and mother tongue behind, the Hebrew culture of Palestine was the clearest expression of the rupture of history, in its personal as well as national dimension. The furious outbreak that followed the Tel Aviv reception for the Yiddish writers cannot be understood outside this sense that Hebraism required the rejection of earlier codes, whether these were the sanctioned domesticity Shlonsky mocked, the maternal embrace Katznelson-Shazar escaped, or the heterosexual decadence over which Greenberg triumphed. The public debate that followed Shlonsky's rejection of the Hebrew-Yiddish "marriage made in heaven," then, marks the end not only of traditional Hebrew-Yiddish bilingualism but also of the Hebrew-Yiddish sexual-linguistic system as a whole. It is curious, therefore, that perhaps the most powerful phrase to describe this system was the metaphor proposed by Bialik and attacked by Shlonsky. The metaphor of Hebrew and Yiddish as husband and wife is, of course, implicit in the structure of Hebrew-Yiddish relations and underlies much of the metadiscourse of this language-culture. Nevertheless, the metaphor broke through to the surface of public discourse only at the moment when the long relationship between the two languages was finally dissolving.

In Conclusion

Our mother tongue has grown old. The mother is already a
grandmother and a great-grandmother. . . . She remembers what
happened fifty years ago better and more clearly than what
happened this morning.

—Isaac Bashevis Singer, 1986

I fell in love with Yiddish when it was very nearly too late, which is a
familiar story. Yiddish was my first language. I think I can remember
absorbing the sense of my own body's preciousness along with the list
by which its parts were named to me: *kepele, oygele, fisele.* Yiddish is also
the language in which I communicated with my grandparents, the language I heard at home and in which my father made something of a
living as a journalist. The Orthodox neighborhood in which I grew up
was a kind of alternate map of Eastern Europe: up the street from us
was the fluorescently lit storefront called Stolin; our backyard bordered
on the back-lot of the blocky brown buildings of Bobov, where a *succah*
that seated a thousand and was decorated with electrified biblical scenes
went up every year; a few blocks over was a brick corner house called
Chernobyl(!), where I held the spicebox for the *havdalah* ceremony before I got too big a girl for my father to take me there. But I don't remember being curious about the places these synagogues memorialized,
as if the very project of remapping Eastern Europe onto Brooklyn—if
that's what was happening—worked to foreclose nostalgia or curiosity.

There was, too, a great deterrent to looking back, since that entailed
looking through a blackness so dense it swallowed everything beyond it.
I knew that by the time I met him, for instance, my father had already
lived a long and complicated life, a good portion of it before the war. But
this was a dark knowledge, really a kind of ignorance apparently not
uncommon among children of survivors. I don't question the decision of
my parents and their friends to keep us from knowledge of "the Holocaust" (the word was always said with an implied snort in our house).
Let the German children see those films, I remember a family friend
saying. But because the end was so unspeakable, we were cut off from
what came before that too.

It isn't so surprising that my parents never tried to stop me from speaking to them in English, even if they answered in Yiddish. They spoke Yiddish, but they weren't Yiddishists. What was important was Israel, and the Jewish people, whatever language they spoke. I was given two names: a Hebrew name that came unencumbered with ancestors and a Yiddish one, Sheindel, after a great-grandmother; my parents called me by the Hebrew one, and I preferred it that way. The Hebrew name, which sounded more "modern" to me, had the ring of Zionist pioneer life. My elementary school offered a Hebrew track and a Yiddish one, and I was glad my parents chose to have me study Hebrew (ivris actually, in the Ashkenazic pronunciation, while "Yiddish" we called "Jewish"), where the teachers were a little younger and the students a shade more worldly. Yiddish was the world where stockings were supposed to have seams, where women wore wigs *and* hats *and* shaved their heads—instead of just the wigs, the way it was done among our particular stripe. Escaping that religious world meant leaving Yiddish behind, and I did it without a backward glance.

My fascination with Jewish Eastern Europe began only long after I'd broken with its New York counterpart. I fell in love with Yiddish far from Brooklyn, at the National Yiddish Book Center in Amherst, the summer I worked as a student intern there. I shelved Sholem Aleichem, wearing five earrings and trading black jokes among the knee-deep piles of Yiddish books we were "saving." (Question: What's the thinnest book in the Yiddish Book Center? Answer: *Jews in Postwar Poland*. Or: *The Joy of Jewish Prayer*.) We were anarchists one and all, followers of Emma Goldman and others whose existence we faintly discerned from the titles we were cataloging. A strange occupation for a group of would-be revolutionaries—curators, conservators, alphabetizers of Yiddish culture, breathing in the decay of old books like Bartleby the Scrivener.

Most of the summer interns had only enough Yiddish to separate fiction from nonfiction, or even just *alef* from *beyz*. Here, my rusty Yiddish was a near-miracle, more thrilling and socially valuable than an ability to speak Latin or juggle. Here, my childhood suddenly seemed colorful and "authentic." No wonder my parents were a little bemused by the friends I brought home, that summer and later, to hear a little Yiddish from someone who hadn't learned it from a book. (My father referred to them collectively as the "Yidishisten," and I jokingly called my forays the "Boro Park Safaris.") It must have struck them as absurd, this belated enthusiasm for the Yiddish I had abandoned, an enthusiasm that manifested itself, moreover, primarily among those for whom Yiddish was fairly exotic. Yiddishists without Yiddish. Well, better a Jew without a beard than a beard without a Jew.

What I discovered at the Book Center, actually, was the *idea* of Yiddish, quite apart from its grammar and usefulness as a medium of expression. It no longer embarrasses me that what I have called my love affair with Yiddish (like Peretz's before me, and Abramovitsh before him, though less heterosexual, I suppose) is so fed by the imaginary, so much the idea of the thing. Part of my argument in this book, after all, is that Hebrew and Yiddish were, besides languages, ideas and perceptions about languages. And these ideas were among the greatest and most powerful of Ashkenazic culture. Dvora Ben-Yehuda's story illustrates, among other things, that people are perfectly capable of a radical, life-altering commitment to a language whose grammar and vocabulary is utterly mysterious to them. And when Nathan Birnbaum was rallying support for an international conference on the Yiddish language in the first decade of this century, he was forced to address audiences in German because he could not manage the Yiddish that so fired his enthusiasm. There is some meaning, then, to "Yiddishism" and "Hebraism" quite apart from mastery of the language.

Yiddish was significant to me because it gave me both my worlds in one paradoxical package: the traditional life and my rebellion against it. What I loved in Yiddish were the books I found in the Book Center rather than the ones on my parents' shelves (which were almost all in Hebrew—or Loshn-koydesh—or English). *Togbukh fun an elende maydl, Hashish.* What I was introduced to in the Book Center, and later at YIVO, was a particular mirroring of my own experience, a culture in which Jewish rebellion found community and expression. There were entire generations in which escape was collective biography and existential condition, in which secularism did not mean falling off the map, as it seemed to in my own experience. The search for subversion ended up taking me to the archives—back, in a sense, to where I had started. If feminism had something to do with my rejection of Orthodoxy, it also led me to the Yiddish prayers of generations of pious Ashkenazic women. This project, then, gave me back both my traditional home and what turned out to be just as traditional—my break with it. George Steiner has written about the "many-centeredness" of the multilingual. Maybe only a book that takes its place between two languages and is written in a third could begin to reflect the experiences I have described.

A Marriage Made in Heaven, in more ways than I can possibly be conscious of, is clearly a product of the circumstances of my own history.

But it also arose in the more general environment of contemporary American Jewish culture. My interest in Hebrew-Yiddish relations does not involve my choosing sides, the way it might have seventy years ago. The "language question" is moot, though not because either side made a better case to the Jewish people or was more firmly committed to its cause. The language debate was prematurely and violently foreclosed by the Nazi murder of half the world's Yiddish speakers and the destruction of Jewish Eastern European life; by Stalin's murder of many others, including the best-known poets, journalists, and actors of Soviet Yiddish culture; by the founding of the state of Israel on the wreckage of Jewish history. Among so much broken glass, so much blood and terror, what point could there be in continuing the debate? Maybe the Hebraists were right that aspirations to make Yiddish a national language of the Jews were wrongheaded or doomed or divisive of the entirety of the Jewish people. But Hebrew has won so utterly that Yiddishist aspirations no longer register as a threat, and their defeat can be mourned even by the formerly most fervent champions of Hebrew.

With Hebrew safely established as the national language of Israel and with the decimation of Yiddish speakers, the relative positions of Hebrew and Yiddish on the Jewish emotional scale have reversed the long historical hierarchy that had governed Hebrew-Yiddish relations. Hebrew is now the language of the street and the (Tel Aviv stock) market; Yiddish, increasingly, is a language of books, a new kind of "holy tongue" accessible only to the old, the most religious segments of the Jewish population, and to a small group of "classicists." As others have ironically commented, Yiddish is the new Loshn-koydesh, Holy Tongue, because it is *lashon hakedoshim*, the language of the holy ones, the martyrs. Yiddish has gained some dignity, attracted some love—even if, as in my case, belatedly. And the historical circumstances that connected Yiddish with women readers in the sixteenth century have a curious corollary in the late twentieth century, when the second wave of Jewish feminism has combined with diaspora ideology (part ethnic nostalgia, part disillusionment with Zionism, part postmodernism) to generate a surge of interest in women and Yiddish, as a recent conference sponsored by the National Council of Jewish Women was entitled.

The conflict between Hebrew and Yiddish may have been overwhelmed by history, but the core of my argument, that these languages represented the masculine and feminine faces of Ashkenazic Jewry, continues to be consequential. It matters, it seems to me, that the language associated with Jewish men has gained dominance, even if now it is equally, or nearly so, the language of women. Hebrew has been shaped by its history, and it continues to shape its speakers, in ways I imply in the last chapter. And Hebrew has triumphed not only in Palestine but also within the culture of American Jews, where it is the language of Hebrew schools and a favored elective of Jewish college students. The Jewish language, now, is the one that connects them with the liturgy and texts of their ancestors and with their Israeli cousins, but not, for the most part, with their grandparents. Students in a beginning Hebrew language class I taught knew the words for God, and blessed, and you (in the masculine, of course, not the feminine); when I asked the class if anyone knew the words for grandmother and grandfather, one student ventured: "Bubby and Zayde?" To say no was to acknowledge the closure of one avenue of Jewish continuity, the irrelevance of one kind of Jewish knowledge. For contemporary American Jews, the Holocaust has not registered as the cultural genocide it also was; the evaporation of social capital, the narrowing of political choice, is everywhere evident but rarely felt.

But our Yiddish amnesia, for reasons this book should begin to explain, is particularly devastating for Ashkenazic women. American Jewish feminists have struggled to make changes in the synagogue and liturgy that would seem mild by comparison with the prayers recited and composed by their grandmothers, but they have struggled with only the barest consciousness of the alternative spiritual expression of traditional Ashkenazic women or of the feminist radicality of writers like Dvora Baron. Yiddish texts can illuminate the experiences of Ashkenazic women, religious and secular, pious and revolutionary (or both).

Shmuel Niger's 1912 essay "Yiddish Literature and the Female Reader" tells as much about the environment in which it was written as it does about the historical period the essay covered. The same, of course, could be said about my own work. Although the narrative I explore ends in the 1920s, the perspective from which it is told was opened up, it seems to me, by developments in postwar Jewish life. This project was partly fueled by the "Yiddish revival" and partly by American Jewish feminism, movements whose connections I hope my work helps to clarify. But my analysis of Hebrew-Yiddish relations was also enabled, in a different way, by the success of the Hebrew revival; the particular critique of Hebraism mounted here has become possible, it seems to me, only insofar as the establishment of Hebrew as a Jewish vernacular is no longer an endangered enterprise.

What dangers remained, it seems to me, derived from my own involvement with the subject. As a feminist and a Yiddishist both, I had to inoculate myself against the very cultural utopianism that was fueling my research, avoiding the phantasm of an "authentic" or "feminine" Yiddish past, the warmth of the maternal embrace, the lure of the margins. I had to resist caricaturing the relations between Hebrew and Jewish men, reminding myself that the most brutal displays of power of the Hebrew-Yiddish language wars were, after all, the suppression of Hebraists by Soviet Yiddishists, not the "masculine" Palestinian Hebraist rhetoric. There were other pitfalls I had to navigate that were less central to my thesis: the persistence of mourning for Yiddish, in which I participate, runs the risk of ignoring that Yiddish is still spoken and lived, and that the Holocaust is not the only explanation for the decline of Yiddish among Ashkenazic Jews. To the extent that the move away from Yiddish was a function of Jewish success, mourning the "death" of Yiddish seems to me to be in bad faith.

There are undoubtedly other blind spots in this work. I comfort myself in this regard by recognizing that the prejudices and imbalances are at least partly the result of an emotional engagement with the subject at hand. The mutual interference between the story told here and my own telling of it may be the surest sign that this story still continues.

Notes

*All translations from the Hebrew and Yiddish are
my own, except where otherwise noted.*

INTRODUCTION

1. It is more correct to speak of Loshn-koydesh than Hebrew in this context
to designate the language of the traditional Jewish canon. Loshn-koydesh com-
prises not only the various strata of Hebrew, including biblical and rabbinic, but
also Aramaic, the earlier Jewish vernacular in which the Talmud is composed.
The term "Yiddish" is equally deceptive, covering a wide range of historically, socially, and territorially diverse forms of the language. Moreover, the
name Yiddish, which has become nearly universally used, was common only
among uneducated people until the first years of this century. Thus, "Hebrew-
Yiddish internal bilingualism" should not be taken to mean a stable or fixed
relation between two distinct languages but rather should be read differently in
each context to which the concept might apply. For a fascinating discussion of
the political implications of the use of different names of Old Yiddish by different historians, see Jerold C. Frakes, *The Politics of Interpretation: Alterity and
Ideology in Old Yiddish Studies* (Albany: State University of New York Press,
1989), 21–103. Max Weinreich, *The History of the Yiddish Language,* trans.
Shlomo Noble and Joshua Fishman (Chicago: University of Chicago Press, [1973]
1980), 320–325, also discusses the various names of Yiddish, including "Yiddish."

2. See Charles A. Ferguson, "Diglossia," *Word* 15 (1959): 325–340. By a
curious coincidence of intellectual history, Ferguson's pioneering description of
the phenomenon of dual-language cultures and Weinreich's description of "internal bilingualism" appeared in the same year.

3. Max Weinreich, "Internal Bilingualism in Ashkenaz until the Haskalah:
Facts and Concepts" [Yiddish], *Goldene keyt* 35 (1959): 3–11.

4. Max Weinreich, "Internal Bilingualism in Ashkenaz," trans. Lucy Davi-

dowicz, in *Voices from the Yiddish,* ed. Irving Howe and Eliezer Greenberg (New York: Schocken Books, [1959] 1975), 279–280. Subsequent references are to this abridged version of the essay.

5. Shmuel Niger, "Yiddish Literature and the Female Reader" [Yiddish], *Der Pinkes* 1 (1912): 106. The essay is reprinted, with one small deletion, in Niger's *Studies in the History of Yiddish Literature* [Yiddish], ed. H. Leivick (New York: Sh. Niger Book Committee, 1959), 35–108. All references are to the 1912 version, unless otherwise noted.

6. Niger, "Yiddish Literature," 91, cites as an early prototype of this formula the 1534 translation of Job, which is directed to "women and the ordinary people who cannot study Torah."

7. Weinreich, *History of the Yiddish Language,* 276.

8. Sh. Z. London, *The Congregation of Shloyme,* 3d ed. (Amsterdam: n.p., 1772), quoted in Niger, "Yiddish Literature," 92.

9. Niger, "Yiddish Literature," 113.

10. Ibid., 121–122.

11. Weinreich, *History of the Yiddish Language,* 277. Weinreich credits the Arabic and Ladino scholar Max Gruenbaum with coining the phrase "women's literature," but he argues that the phrase is not completely accurate. For an American-Jewish feminist treatment of this literature, see Chava Weissler, "The Traditional Piety of Ashkenazic Women," *Jewish Spirituality II,* ed. Arthur Green (New York: Crossroad Press, 1989), 245–275. See, as well, Dorothy Bilik's paper on Niger, "Prematurely Politically Correct," presented at the annual conference of the Modern Language Association, San Francisco, 1991.

12. Niger, "Yiddish Literature," 130. Significantly, the term "vayber-taytsh," or women's Yiddish, is often used interchangeably with "ivre-taytsh" to describe the distinctive language and style of the premodern Yiddish translations of Hebrew source texts. Yiddish books published until the nineteenth century were virtually all typeset in the rounded letters known as "taytsh" or "vayber-taytsh." For a discussion of the history of these terms as well as the typographical shifts that visually accompanied them, see Weinreich, *History of the Yiddish Language,* 263, 275.

13. Niger's plans to rework his early essay on Yiddish and the female reader as well as his proposal for a sequel to the essay are discussed in Yitshak Rifkind, "Afterword," in Shmuel Niger, *Studies in the History,* 431–438. According to Rifkind, Niger assembled material to support his arguments (which remained relatively unchanged) over the course of his lifetime but never managed to incorporate this material into the essay. Niger's two articles in effect split the category of "women and the common people" to whom Yiddish literature of the sixteenth and seventeenth centuries was often addressed. The separation of these conflated groups into two (which is reflected in my own work) may have had the advantage of reversing what was felt to be the feminization of the Jewish masses. Note that Niger uses the term "folk" rather than "proste mentshen" (common people), although the latter is typical of Yiddish authors' addresses. Implicit in his use of the term "folk" is the valorization of a previously denigrated category, akin, perhaps, to Niger's partial and problematic transvaluation of the feminine in his first study.

14. The French feminist critic Hélène Cixous, "Sorties," trans. Ann Liddle, in *New French Feminisms: An Anthology*, ed. Elaine Marks and Isabelle de Courtivron (New York: Schocken Books, [1975] 1980), 91, argues that such binary oppositions are common to all patriarchal philosophical systems.

Wherever an ordering intervenes, a law organizes the thinkable by (dual, irreconcilable; or mitigable, dialectical) oppositions. And all the couples of oppositions are *couples*. Does this mean something? Is the fact that logocentrism subjects thought—all of the concepts, the codes, the values—to a two-term system, related to "the" couple, man/woman?

15. Christopher Hutton, "Freud and the Family Drama of Yiddish," in *Studies in Yiddish Linguistics*, ed. Paul Wexler (Tübingen: Niemeyer Press, 1990), 10.

16. The situation of the Ben-Yehuda family, in which the wife acquired foreign languages earlier than the husband, while he knew Hebrew from an early age, appears to be typical of young Eastern European Jews of the Haskalah period and later. This gendering of multilingualism in the nineteenth and early twentieth century has some characteristics in common with the earlier patterns of Jewish bilingualism. Just as women were more likely to read Yiddish books than their brothers or husbands, Jewish women may have been earlier and more commonly exposed to non-Jewish languages than their male counterparts, whose educational environment demanded a stricter commitment to Hebrew and Aramaic religious texts. Ben-Yehuda's tutelage by his future wife, Dvora Yonas, is recounted in Itamar Ben-Avi, "Introduction," in *The Complete Works of Eliezer Ben-Yehuda* [Hebrew], ed. Itamar Ben-Avi (Jerusalem: Bialik Institute, 1941), 7.

17. Sander Gilman, *Jewish Self-Hatred: Antisemitism and the Secret Language of the Jews* (Baltimore: Johns Hopkins University Press, 1986), 200. Hutton, "Freud and the Family Drama," 21, makes similar claims for Yiddish's "femininity" vis-à-vis German, although he does not link this gendering of Yiddish with the self-hatred of the assimilated male Jew who perceives himself as emasculated, as Gilman does. Instead, he more positively views the connections between Yiddish and the feminine in Freud's thought in the light of Freud's theories of sexuality and socialization: "It does seem evident . . . that in adopting German culture Freud felt that he had denied the authentic and intimate, and in this sense, the natural, the feminine and the sexual in his nature, this being in part symbolized by Yiddish." It seems likely that the relations between German and Yiddish, in contrast with those that connect Hebrew and Yiddish, are largely a reflection of ethnic and social differences (between Germans and Jews and between German Jews and Eastern European Jews).

18. Sandra M. Gilbert and Susan Gubar, *No Man's Land*. Vol. 1: *The War of the Words* (New Haven: Yale University Press, 1988), 243.

19. The clearest and most direct description of this concept can be found in Jacques Lacan, "On the Possible Treatment of Psychosis," in *Ecrits: A Selection*, trans. Alan Sheridan (New York: W. W. Norton, [1966] 1977), 218: "What I do wish to insist on is that we should concern ourselves not only with the way the mother accommodates herself to the person of the father, but also with the way she takes his speech, the word (*mot*), let us say, of his authority, in other words, of the place that she reserves for the Name-of-the-Father in the promulgation

of the law." Lacan's "insistence" on our hearing *his* "word" as well as his ahistorical and apolitical view of patriarchal authority should explain the challenge of his work to contemporary French feminists.

20. Hélène Cixous, "*Sorties:* Out and Out: Attacks/Ways Out/Forays," trans. Betsy Wing, in *The Feminist Reader: Essays in Gender and the Politics of Literary Criticism*, ed. Catherine Belsey and Jane Moore (New York: Basil Blackwell, [1975] 1989), 111.

21. Michel Foucault, "What Is an Author?" in *Textual Strategies*, ed. J. Harari (Ithaca: Cornell University Press, [1969] 1979), 141–160.

22. George Steiner, *After Babel: Aspects of Language and Translation* (London, Oxford, New York: Oxford University Press, 1975), 116.

CHAPTER 1. ENGENDERING AUDIENCES

1. Sholem Aleichem, "Last Will and Testament," in *Sholom Aleichem Panorama*, ed. Melech Grafstein (London: Jewish Observer Press, 1948), 184. The will reads, in part,

No matter where I die, I am to be buried not among aristocrats, people of high lineage, or people of great wealth, but among common Jewish workers, just ordinary folk; so that the tombstone to be put up on my grave will honor the ordinary graves around mine, and the ordinary graves will honor my tombstone, in the way in which the plain, honest people honored their folk writer in his lifetime.

2. Sholem Aleichem, "Epitaph" [Yiddish], *Ale verk fun Sholem Aleichem*, vol. 2 (Moscow: Emes Press, 1948), 284. A Hebrew version of the epitaph, which is a near but not exact translation of the epitaph, is inscribed on the back of the gravestone. The translation was probably done by the writer's son-in-law, a Hebrew writer in his own right named I. D. Berkowitz, who also translated many of his father-in-law's works into Hebrew.

3. "The writer's audience is always a fiction," writes Walter Ong in *The Presence of the Word* (New Haven: Yale University Press, 1967), 116. Ong analyzes writers' modes of projecting a collective consciousness onto their readership and recounts the history of the ways in which audiences have been called on to fictionalize themselves.

4. Niger, "Yiddish Literature," 100.

5. Ibid.

6. Moshe Altshuler, *Burning Mirror* [Yiddish] (1596), as quoted in Chava Weissler, "For Women and for Men Who Are Like Women: The Construction of Gender in Yiddish Devotional Literature," *Journal of Feminist Studies in Religion* 5, no. 2 (1989): 9.

7. Weissler, "For Women and for Men Who Are Like Women," 12.

8. Weinreich, *History of the Yiddish Language*, 277.

9. In a fascinating aside, Niger, "Yiddish Literature and the Female Reader," 127 n. 139, describes a visit to a well-known maskil, Yehoshua Mazeh. He asked the older man whether he knew the identity of this new "Sarah Bas-Tovim" who had recently published a collection of modern tkhines. Mazeh brought Niger over to the mirror, pointed to the reflection of his own wizened face, and said, "There

she is." Niger also cites the rumor that the Yiddish novelist I. M. Dik was among those publishing tkhines under the pseudonym "Sarah Bas-Tovim." There is at least one irony to be noted here: Sore Bas-Tovim (who was long considered a legendary figure but is now believed to have lived in the eighteenth century) adopted a pen name (literally "daughter of good men" or, idiomatically, "women of good lineage") and cited a long patrilineage to establish herself as a member of a distinguished family of male rabbis, while, less than two hundred years later, scholarly Jewish men would take her name not only to hide their indulgence in "womanly pursuits" but also as a proud sign of their affiliation with a well-known woman writer. For the historical debate on Bas-Tovim, see Dr. Israel Tsinberg, *Old Yiddish Literature*, in *The History of the Jewish Literature*, vol. 6 (New York: Sklarsky Press, 1943), 286–289.

10. Sholem Yankev Abramovitsh, "Notes for My Literary Biography" [Hebrew], in *The Complete Works of Mendele Mokher Sforim* (Tel Aviv: Dvir Press, 1958), 4.

11. Niger, "Yiddish Literature," 121–122.

12. See Isaac Meir Dik, "Introduction," in *A Play vs. a Play* [Yiddish] (Warsaw: n.p., 1861), 4, as quoted in David Roskies, *A Bridge of Longing: The Lost Art of Yiddish Storytelling* (Cambridge, Mass.: Harvard University Press, 1995), 67. For a discussion of I. M. Dik's authorial addresses as well as a sociological analysis of his reading public, see Max Weinreich, "Isaac Meir Dik," in *Studies in Yiddish Literary History* [Yiddish] (Vilna: Tomer Press, 1928), 299–300.

13. Niger, "Yiddish Literature from the Mid-Eighteenth Century until 1942," in *Universal Encyclopedia*, vol. 3: *Jews* (New York: CYCO Press, 1942), 101, as quoted in Ken Frieden, *Classic Yiddish Fiction: Abramovitsh, Sholem Aleichem, and Peretz* (Albany: State University of New York Press, 1995), 17.

14. Isaac Meir Dik, "Words of Righteousness" [Yiddish], (Vilna: Fin-Rozenkrantz, 1863), 41–42, as quoted in David Roskies, "Dik's Bibliography," in *The Field of Yiddish: Studies in Language, Folklore, and Literature, Fourth Collection*, ed. Marvin Herzog, Barbara Kirshenblatt-Gimblett, Dan Miron, and Ruth Wisse (Philadelphia: Institute for the Study of Human Issues, 1980), 119.

15. Isaac Meir Dik, *The Women Shopkeepers, or Golde Mine the Abandoned Wife of Brod* [Yiddish] (Vilna: Fin-Rozenkrantz, 1865), iii.

16. A. Y. Papirna, as quoted in Shmuel Niger, "Isaac Meir Dik: Biographical-Critical Notes" [Yiddish], in *The Selected Works* (New York: Congress for Jewish Cultures, 1954), viii.

17. Isaac Meir Dik, *American Story* [Yiddish], vol. 1 (Vilna: n.p., 1899); reprinted in Niger, "Yiddish Literature," 116–117.

18. This perception is not unique to the Yiddish Haskalah movement. Many Hebrew Haskalah writers also suggested that women might be the conduit to an overall Jewish acceptance of Enlightenment ideology through the instruction of Hebrew in an environment free of the "medievalism" of the traditional male educational institutions. Moreover, agitating against the oppression of women in traditional Judaism was an important goal or strategy for the Haskalah, in its Hebrew as well as its Yiddish manifestations.

19. For an analysis of female readership in the nineteenth century, and more specifically of the effects of the Enlightenment on Jewish women, see Iris

Parush, "Readers in Cameo: Women Readers in Jewish Society in Nineteenth-Century Eastern Europe," *Prooftexts* 14, no. 1 (January 1994): 1–24.

20. I. J. Trunk, *Poland: Memories and Images* [Yiddish] (New York: Undzer Tsayt Press, 1947), 2:54. Quoted in Parush, "Readers in Cameo," 7.

21. Abramovitsh, "Notes toward My Literary Biography," 5.

22. Dan Miron, *A Traveler Disguised: A Study in the Rise of Modern Yiddish Fiction in the Nineteenth Century* (New York: Schocken Books, 1973), 90–94, 115–118, reads the creation of the Mendele persona as a function of the tension between these two sorts of concerns, the first demanding the writer's engagement with his audience and the second inviting his distance and self-concealment.

23. Weissler, "For Women and for Men Who Are Like Women," 11.

24. Yehuda Leyb Gordon, *Songs of Wisdom, Parables and Narrative Poems* [Hebrew], ed. Moshe Mahler and David Niger (Jerusalem and Tel Aviv: Schocken Press, 1965), 3.

25. Miron, *A Traveler Disguised*, 3.

26. This view of later generations' assessment of the Haskalah movement, particularly its Hebrew branch, is expounded in Michael Stanislawski's introduction to his biography of Gordon, entitled *For Whom Do I Toil?* (New York and Oxford: Oxford University Press, 1988). On page 6, Stanislawski notes that while most modern Jewish historians have been either Zionists or Socialists, and therefore unsympathetic with "Judah Leyb Gordon and other proponents of a gradual, liberal, sanguine transformation of the life and culture of the Jews of Eastern Europe," the consensus that "Judah Leyb Gordon was simply too shortsighted or narrow-minded" may be correct.

27. Yehuda Leyb Gordon, "For Whom Do I Toil?" [Hebrew], in *The Complete Works of Yehuda Leyb Gordon: Poetry* (Tel Aviv: Dvir Press, [1870] 1960), 27.

28. Gordon, *Complete Works*, 18.

29. Yehuda Leyb Gordon, "The Tip of the Yod" [1875, Hebrew], in *The Complete Works*, 129–139.

30. Yosef Klausner, *A History of Modern Hebrew Literature* [Hebrew], 6 vols. (Jerusalem, 1930–1960), 6:388.

31. Parush, "Readers in Cameo," 17.

32. Ibid., 16.

33. For a historical account of the suppression of Hebrew in the Soviet Union, see Yehoshua A. Gilboa, *Fight for Survival: Hebrew Culture in the Soviet Union* [Hebrew] (Tel Aviv: Sifri'at hapo'alim, 1977).

34. "A Weak Position for a Strong Complaint," cartoon, *Der groyser kundes*, 30 August 1926, as reproduced in *Never Say Die: A Thousand Years of Yiddish Life and Letters*, ed. Joshua A. Fishman (The Hague: Mouton Press, 1981), 421. *Der groyser kundes: A zhornal far humor, vits, un satire* (The Big Prankster: A Journal of Humor, Jest, and Satire), was edited by Jacob Marinoff and appeared from 1909 to 1928, first as a monthly, then as a biweekly, and ultimately every week. For a description of the publication history of *Der groyser kundes*, including its beginnings as a monthly entitled *Der kibitzer*, some of its frequent contributors, and its circulation (from 18,000 to a peak of 35,000 weekly), see

Y. Chaykin, *The Yiddish Press in America* [Yiddish] (New York: Shklarski Press, 1946), 210–214.

35. Joshua A. Fishman, "Cartoons about Language: Hebrew, Yiddish, and the Visual Representation of Sociolinguistic Attitudes," in *Hebrew in Ashkenaz: A Language in Exile*, ed. Lewis Glinert (New York and Oxford: Oxford University Press, 1993), 154–155.

36. Benjamin Harshav, *The Meaning of Yiddish* (Berkeley, Los Angeles, London: University of California Press, 1990), 23.

37. Weinreich, *History of the Yiddish Language*, 270–271.

38. While the cartoons about Hebrew and Yiddish and the term "mame-loshn" call on firmly embedded cultural myths, the polemical uses to which they put these myths are distinctively modern. In fact, the matronym "mame-loshn," for all its folksy flavor, appears in writing, according to Max Weinreich, "perhaps no earlier than the beginning of the twentieth century." The celebration of the historical associations between Yiddish and Jewish women, then, appears to be a relatively recent phenomenon, dating from roughly the same time that Yiddish was attaining status as a recognized language. Weinreich, *History of the Yiddish Language*, 271.

39. "No! It's a Legitimate Love Affair!" cartoon, *Der groyser kundes*, 5 February 1926, as reproduced in Fishman, *Never Say Die*, 133.

40. "Y. L. Peretz's Popular Novel," cartoon, *Der groyser kundes*, 16 June 1911, as reproduced in Fishman, *Never Say Die*, 468.

41. *Der Yidisher Arbeter*, 10 September 1908, as quoted in *The First Yiddish Language Conference* [Yiddish], (Vilna: YIVO Press, 1931), 205.

42. *The First Yiddish Language Conference*, 79.

43. Ibid.

44. Chayim Nachman Bialik, letter to Sholem Aleichem, in *The Bialik Book* [Hebrew], ed. Y. Fichman (Tel Aviv: Dvir Press, 1934), 93.

45. Robert Alter, *The Invention of Hebrew Prose* (Seattle: University of Washington Press, 1988), 9–10, discusses the class background of Hebrew and Yiddish writers in some detail, concluding that these writers came from all rungs of society with one notable exception, the Socialist youth who gravitated toward Yiddish in their "programmatic renegotiation of the terms of collective existence" (p. 10).

46. Chaim Grade, *My Mother's Sabbaths* [Yiddish] (New York: CYCO Press, 1959), 14.

47. Weinreich, *History of the Yiddish Language*, 277.

CHAPTER 2. THE TRANSSEXUAL IMAGINATION

1. David Frishman, "Mendele: His Life and Work" [Yiddish], in *The Complete Works of Mendele Mokher Sforim: Criticism*, vol. 10 (New York: Hebrew Publishing Company, [1910] 1920), 56.

Abramovitsh's 1909 journey is also described in detail in *The Mendele Book*, ed. Nachman Mayzel (New York: Yidisher Kultur Farband, 1959), 421–427. This description includes newspaper reports and eyewitness reminiscences that corroborate Frishman's account.

2. Bal Machshoves [I. Elyashiv], "A Grandson of the Grandfather" [Yiddish], in *Complete Works of Mendele Mokher Sforim,* 10:61–62.

3. Shmuel Niger, *Mendele Mokher Sforim: His Life, His Social and Literary Achievements* [Yiddish] (New York: Ikuf Press, 1970), 7. Shmuel Niger, *The Bilingualism of Our Literature* [Yiddish] (Detroit: Posy Shoulson Press, 1941), 84–85, develops the analogy between the "zogerke" (sometimes called *firzogerin*) and early Yiddish literature, which functioned as a mediator between the Hebrew literary tradition and the common people. The reference to Abramovitsh as writing in a masculine Jewish tradition recurs in various critical texts, including Micha Yosef Berditshevski's entitling of Abramovitsh the "Maimonides of Yiddish literature" (Micha Yosef Berditshevski, "Mendele," in *Yiddish Writings of a Distant Relative* [Yiddish] [New York: Ikuf Press, 1951], 184–186); and Yankev Glatshteyn's discussion of Abramovitsh's pieces as *gmorelakh,* or talmudic pieces, in Yankev Glatshteyn, *Basically Speaking* [Yiddish] (New York: Matones Press, 1956), 11 ff.

4. Dan Miron, *A Traveler Disguised,* 30–32, describes how, in dedicating his first novel *Stempenyu* to Sh. Y. Abramovitsh, Sholem Aleichem crowned his more established colleague the "zayde" or "grandfather" of Yiddish literature. As Miron points out, Sholem Aleichem was twenty-nine years old in 1888 when *Stempenyu* first appeared, while Abramovitsh was no more than fifty-two. In Miron's assessment, Sholem Aleichem's reference to Abramovitsh as a "grandfather" was a deliberately mythologizing construction, exaggerating Abramovitsh's age to camouflage

the shortness and scantiness of the tradition [Sholem Aleichem] was fabricating: By the adoption of Abramovitsh as a "grandfather," however, [Sholem Aleichem] gained for Yiddish literature much more than the dignity of old age; he supplied it with a living symbol of authority and legitimacy. The grandfather myth obviously involved myths of a grandson and of an inheritance, in short, of a dynasty. Once Abramovitsh was accepted as a reigning sire, it went without saying that only his legitimate progeny were to inherit the kingdom; moreover, it also became evident that a kingdom did exist; a kingdom which had a past and was looking toward a future. (pp. 30–31)

5. The Hebrew version is similar but makes no reference to Hebrew or Yiddish writers. Mendele never explains his inferiority to the writers, "acheynu hasofrim."

6. Abramovitsh, "Notes toward My Literary Biography," 4–5.

7. Elizabeth Kloty Beaujour, *Alien Tongues: Bilingual Russian Writers of the "First" Emigration* (Ithaca: Cornell University Press, 1989), notes the prevalence of guilt feelings in her subjects, Russian writers who turned to another language after leaving Russia: "Depending on who they are, on the circumstances of their relations to their various languages, and in what period of their careers they find themselves, bilingual writers may express their linguistic situation in terms of bigamy, adultery, or incest" (p. 89).

8. Abramovitsh, "Notes toward My Literary Biography," 4.

9. Miron, *A Traveler Disguised,* 14.

10. Abramovitsh, "Notes toward My Literary Biography," 4.

11. Gordon, *Songs of Reason*, 6.

12. Miron, *A Traveler Disguised*, 14.

13. Abramovitsh, "Notes toward My Literary Biography," 5.

14. Weinreich, "Isaac Meir Dik," esp. pp. 299–300.

15. Abramovitsh, *The Little Person* [Yiddish and Hebrew], ed. and trans. Shalom Luria (Haifa: Haifa University Press, [1864] 1984), 52. Luria reprints the earliest 1864 (Yiddish) edition of *Dos kleyne mentshele* with a Hebrew translation on facing pages.

16. Ibid., 118.

17. See, for example, Shmuel Niger, "Sholem Yankev Abramovitsh," in *The Complete Works of Mendele Mokher Sforim*, vol. 1 (Warsaw: "Mendele" Press, 1927), 114, where he describes the different attitudes toward Hebrew and Yiddish among maskilic writers: "Even those who weighed every word in Hebrew, trying to 'purify the language' just chattered in Yiddish, half-German, Polish-Russian. Yiddish was the language of the marketplace, of the kitchen; there was no one with whom to have a gentlemanly conversation." Kitchen and food analogies for Yiddish are rather more widespread than the phrase "kitchen language" itself. Abramovitsh, for example, refers to Mendele as a writer/cook in the introduction to *The Travels*. Yankev Dinezon, *Memories and Portraits* [Yiddish] (Warsaw: Ahisefer, 1928), 184, relates a conversation in which Dinezon asked a bookseller why Abramovitsh had left his Yiddish work unsigned. The bookseller answered that signing his name to such ivre-taytsh books would be "like covering the borsht in the kitchen with your only *shabes* cloth, which you use for covering the challah."

18. Abramovitsh, *The Little Person*, 52–53.

19. Ibid., 54–56.

20. Ibid., 92.

21. David Eynhorn, "Mendele at Work" [Yiddish], in *The Complete Works of Mendele Mokher Sforim*, vol. 20 (Warsaw: Farlag Mendele, 1928), 59.

22. The Hebrew version of *The Travels of Benjamin the Third* appeared in 1896.

23. Sh. Y. Abramovitsh, "In the Days of the Noise" [Hebrew], in *The Complete Works of Mendele Mokher Sforim* (Tel Aviv: Dvir Press, 1894), 413.

24. "In the Days of the Noise," 415.

25. "In the Days of the Noise," 415. The description here is a grotesque activation of the feminine metaphor Bialik would later use for the revival of Hebrew as living speech, *chevlay leydah*, language pangs.

26. Achad Ha'am [pseudonym for Asher Ginzberg], "The Language Conflict" [Hebrew], in *At a Crossroads*, vol. 2 (Tel Aviv: Dvir Press, [1900] 1961), 301, writes that even women and the poor who knew no Hebrew always felt that Yiddish, the "borrowed tongue," was no more than "a tool for daily use" and "never felt any special love for it."

27. A complete bibliographical index of Abramovitsh's publications in both Hebrew and Yiddish can be found in *Mendele Mokher Sforim: Bibliography of His Works and Letters for the Academic Edition*, ed. Khone Shmeruk and Shmuel Werses (Jerusalem: Hebrew University of Jerusalem, Institute of Jewish Studies'

Mendele Project, 1965). The Hebrew introduction of *Of Bygone Days*, entitled "Petichta demendele moykher sforim," appeared in *Pardes* 2 (Odessa, 1894), 173–188. The Yiddish versions of chapters 4 and 5, which were the next installments to appear, followed throughout the first year of publication of the Yiddish periodical *Der Yud* (1–3, 5–8, 10, 14–15, 19).

28. While the original Hebrew version seems to indicate that both Reb Shloyme and his writer-guests are meant to be Hebrew writers (Reb Shloyme is referred to as *hayisroeli*, the Israelite), the later Yiddish version refers to Reb Shloyme as Shloyme Reb Chayims, as in the title, and to the writers as *yidishe shraybers* (i.e., Jewish/Yiddish writers). The English translation, which follows the Hebrew version of the preface, calls the group "Hebrew writers," although Ruth Wisse, ed., *A Shtetl and Other Yiddish Novellas* (Detroit: Wayne State University Press, 1986), describes in a footnote to this passage Abramovitsh's circle of friends, which included both Yiddish writers (Dubnov, for instance) and the central ideologue of Hebraism, Achad Ha'am (Asher Ginzberg).

29. Sh. Y. Abramovitsh, *The Complete Works of Mendele Mokher Sforim*, vol. 5 [Yiddish], ed. A. Gurshteyn, M. Wiener, and Y. Nusyanov (Moscow: "Emes" Press, 1935), 63.

30. Abramovitsh, *The Complete Works of Mendele Mokher Sforim* [Hebrew], 256.

31. The irony in this critique of masculine literary culture, we should note, is different from describing women participating in a game as joining in the minyan (prayer quorum). The ironic glance at the scholars' self-importance is not shared by them, while the ordinary person may well share the still-subversive humor of describing a mixed-sex party as a defiance of the religious injunction to exclude women from a minyan.

32. Abramovitsh, *Of Bygone Days*, 268.

33. Sholem Yankev Abramovitsh, *Shloyme the Son of Chayim* [Yiddish], in *The Complete Works of Mendele Mokher-Sforim*, vol. 18 (Warsaw: "Mendele" Press, 1936), 37.

34. Ibid., 36.

35. Ibid., 36–37.

36. Rabbi Meir of Rotenberg (d. 1293) questioned the validity of praying in any form other than directly to God. The folk practice of asking ancestors to intercede for the living continued despite these admonitions. See Herman Pollack, *Jewish Folkways in Germanic Lands (1648–1806)* (Cambridge, Mass.: MIT Press, 1971), 49.

37. Abramovitsh, *Of Bygone Days*, 271.

38. See Weissler, "The Traditional Spirituality of Ashkenazic Women," in *Jewish Spirituality II*, ed. Arthur Green (New York: Crossroad Press, 1989), 246, for a citation of the Sarah Bas-Tovim prayer.

CHAPTER 3. BARON "IN THE CLOSET"

1. Moshe Gitlin, "In Her Youth: Memories of a Fellow Townsman" [Hebrew], in *By the Way*, ed. H. Shabta'it [Tsipora Aharanovitsh] (Merchavia: Sifriyat Po'alim, 1960), 208–209.

2. Tsipora Aharonovitsh, "Materials toward a Biography" [Hebrew], in *By the Way*, 7.

3. Nurit Govrin, *The First Half: Dvora Baron, Her Life and Works (1902–1921)* [Hebrew] (Jerusalem: Mosad Bialik, 1988), 28.

4. Shlomo Grodzanski, "Dvora Baron: The Narrated Life" [Hebrew], in *Autobiography of a Reader* (Tel Aviv: Hakibuts Hame'uchad Press, [1956] 1965), 94.

5. Amalia Kahana-Carmon, "The Song of the Bats in Flights," trans. Naomi Sokoloff and Sonia Grober, in *Gender and Text in Modern Hebrew and Yiddish Literature*, ed. Naomi B. Sokoloff, Anne Lapidus Lerner, and Anita Norich (New York and Jerusalem: Jewish Theological Seminary, [1989] 1992), 237.

6. For a detailed example of this collective biography, reconstructing the social milieu and class background of the future Hebrew writer, the texts he might have covered in yeshiva, his linguistic acumen, etc., see Alter, *The Invention of Hebrew Prose*, 7–10.

7. Alan Mintz, *"Banished from Their Father's Table": Loss of Faith and Hebrew Autobiography* (Bloomington and Indianapolis: Indiana University Press, 1989), 4.

8. Govrin, *The First Half*, 204.

9. Gershon Shaked, *Hebrew Fiction 1880–1970: 1. In the Diaspora* [Hebrew] (Tel Aviv: Hakibuts Hame'uchad Press, 1978), 167.

10. Dvora Baron, "Three Sisters" [Hebrew], *Hamelits* 29 (1903), reprinted in Govrin, *The First Half*, 360–363.

11. Govrin, *The First Half*, 101.

12. Dvora Baron, "In the Beginning" [Hebrew], in *Stories* (Tel Aviv: Davar, 1927).

13. Ibid., 7.

14. Ibid., 8.

15. Ibid., 7.

16. "The First Day" [Hebrew] appeared in *Stories* as the third story of the collection, after "In the Beginning" and "Burial."

17. Dvora Baron, "The First Day," in *Stories*, 30.

18. Ibid., 27.

19. Critics, for instance, often note the irony implicit in Tevye's "mistranslations" of Hebrew texts. Harshav, *The Meaning of Yiddish*, 35, sees the Hebrew-Yiddish ironic relationship as a general characteristic of their intertextual connection.

20. Dvora Baron, "Family" [Hebrew], in *What Once Was* (Tel Aviv: Davar Press, 1939), 26.

21. Ibid. The Hebrew highlights Batya's appropriation of masculine power in the term *mezuyenet* (armed), the root of which is *zayin*—weapon.

22. Ibid.

23. Ibid., 34.

24. Ibid., 31.

25. Ibid., 34.

26. Ibid.

27. Michael Stanislawski, *For Whom Do I Toil?* 125.

28. Gordon, *Songs of Thought, Parables, Ballads*, 167–168.

29. Dvora Baron, "Agunah" [Hebrew], in *Stories.*

30. Ibid., 221.

31. "A time is coming—declares my Lord God—when I will send a famine upon the land: not a hunger for bread or a thirst for water, but for hearing the words of the Lord" (Amos 8:11). Amos's prophecy is among the best known of the comparisons of bread and "the words of the Lord."

32. "Agunah," 224.

33. Sh. Niger, "Yiddish Literature and the Female Reader," 124, describes the Yiddish women's Bible, the *Tsenerene,* as the "agadah" (the homiletic or narrative material) to the traditional texts' "halakha" (the legal material).

34. This is not to suggest that women's texts (i.e., religious books written either by or for women) were free of allegoric commentary. Certainly, the *Tsenerene* is a pastiche of midrashic quotation. Moreover, masculine textual practice often overlapped with and contributed to the familiar women's Bibles and tkhines. Nevertheless, femininely marked textual hermeneutics tended to keep closer to the literal level of the narrative, giving additional details about situations and characters or supplying the moral to be learned from these situations (especially as they concern women) rather than suggesting allegorical interpretations.

35. Sh. Y. Agnon, "Agunot" [Hebrew] (1908), 100.

36. Marc Bernstein, in an unpublished paper presented at the NAPH conference, 1 June 1992, entitled "Midrash and Marginality: The 'Agunot' of Dvora Baron and S. Y. Agnon," compares the two stories in the following way:

Baron rejects [Agnon's] universalization that for her trivializes and appropriates the specific experience of female marginality. For Baron, within the exile of the Jewish people, there is a further internal exile of women that reflects the inequity of the power relationship between the sexes. *Aginut* and exile have nothing to do with romantic notions of potential mates wandering in search of each other; instead, these conditions are inscribed in the social position of women.

37. Dvora Baron, "Burial" [Hebrew], *Hachaver* (13–15 March 1908), reprinted in Govrin, *The First Half,* 426.

38. Govrin, *The First Half,* 11.

39. *By the Way,* 9–10.

40. Zrubavel, "With Mendele Moykher Sforim," in *Leaves of Life* [Hebrew] (Tel Aviv: Perets Press, 1960), 228–232. Reprinted in *The Mendele Book* [Yiddish], 427, and excerpted in Govrin, *The First Half,* 77.

41. "Material toward a Literary Biography," 7.

42. In *By the Way,* 209–222, Barukh Ben-Yehuda, a participant in the Zionist, Hebrew-speaking youth group Baron led in Mariampol in 1907, describes the overheated political atmosphere of the town and the divisions between the Yiddish-speaking Bundists and the smaller group determined to learn Hebrew and realize the Zionist dream. Other sources confirm the typicality of this description.

43. "Kadisha" appeared in *Hachaver: A Daily Newspaper for Youth and All Jewish People,* 1:72 (Vilna, 1908); "Kaddish" in *Der Yidisher Arbeter: A Weekly,* 7:15 (Lvov, 1910); "Sister" in *Ha'olam,* 4:31 (Vilna, 1910); "Burial" in *Hachaver,*

1:95 (Vilna, 1908); "An Only Daughter" in *Ney yor: A Literary Collection for the Coming Holidays* (New York, 1909); the Hebrew "Grandma Henya" in *Ha'olam*, 3:33 (Vilna, 1909); and the Yiddish "Grandma Henya" in *Yugend: A Literary Collection*, no. 1 (Stanislavy, 1910). For this and all other publication information, see the bibliographical notes in Govrin, *The First Half*, 313–325.

44. Govrin, *The First Half*, 510.

45. Ibid., 654.

46. Ibid., 466.

47. Ibid., 459.

48. Ibid., 467.

49. Ibid., 660.

50. "Kadish," in Govrin, *The First Half*, 669.

51. "Kadisha," in Govrin, *The First Half*, 419.

CHAPTER 4. A STORMY DIVORCE

1. See Jack Fellman, *The Revival of a Classical Tongue: Eliezer Ben-Yehuda and the Modern Hebrew Language* (The Hague: Mouton, 1973). Although Alter, *The Invention of Hebrew Prose*, does not explicitly discuss Ben-Yehuda's role in the revival of Hebrew as a spoken language, his study of the rise of Hebrew prose presents various ways in which Hebrew prose discovered or invented Hebrew style, idiom, and vocabulary for its own purposes—before, during, and after Ben-Yehuda's work. Alter traces these capacities to an educational system that could provide the basic tools for the creation of a realism "without vernacular," but that helped lay the groundwork for the vernacular revival.

2. Benjamin Harshav, *Language in Time of Revolution* (Berkeley: University of California Press, 1993), 84.

3. Eliezer Ben-Yehuda, *The Dream and Its Fulfillment* [Hebrew], ed. Re'uven Sivan (Jerusalem: Mosad Bialik, 1978), 129–130.

4. Ibid., 9–10.

5. Of course, the phrase "the father of the Hebrew revival" is the English rather than the Hebrew term for Ben-Yehuda's role in reviving Hebrew. In Hebrew, he is called by the quasi-divine name of "mechaye hasafah," the "reviver" of the language. Nevertheless, references to Ben-Yehuda's paternal role are ubiquitous in his own and in other writings on his contribution to the revival.

6. Ben-Yehuda, *The Dream and Its Fulfillment*, 83.

7. Ibid., 26.

8. Amos Elon, *The Israelis: Founder and Sons* (Middlesex: Penguin, 1971), 97. Elon's account draws from Ben-Yehuda's memoirs as well as those of his friends and acquaintances. A synopsis of these narratives can be found in Fellman, *The Revival*, 35–38.

9. Elon, *The Israelis*, 110.

10. Chemda Ben-Yehuda, *Ben-Yehuda: His Life and Project* [Hebrew] (Jerusalem: Ben-Yehuda Press, 1940), 13. The story is also recounted in Robert St.-John, *Tongue of the Prophets: The Life Story of Eliezer Ben-Yehuda* (New York: Doubleday, 1952), 94. St.-John derives his material from English translations of

Eliezer and Chemda Ben-Yehuda's memoirs as well as from personal interviews with surviving members of the Ben-Yehuda family, including Chemda.

11. Chemda Ben-Yehuda, *Ben-Yehuda*, 12.

12. Ben-Yehuda, *The Dream and Its Fulfillment*, 131.

13. Ibid., 57.

14. Fellman, *The Revival*, 58. Fellman reports Professor Rivlin's impressions of the Ben-Yehuda household, as relayed in a personal conversation between Rivlin and Fellman.

15. Itamar Ben-Avi, *With the Dawn of Our Homeland: Memoirs of the First Hebrew Child* [Hebrew] (Jerusalem: Organization for the Publication of the Writings of Itamar Ben-Avi, 1961), 11.

16. Itamar Ben-Avi, *Dawn of Our Homeland*, 14.

17. Avrom Golomb, "People and Language: Jewish Nationality and Yiddish Language" [Yiddish], in *Yearbook of the New Jewish School in Mexico, I. L. Perets* (1962). Reprinted in *Never Say Die*, 152.

18. Itamar Ben-Avi, "The Hebrew Tongue on Women's Lips," 1928, pamphlet (doc. A 43/104, Central Zionist Archives), 1.

19. For a collection of essays on women's contributions to the settling of Palestine, the Hebrew revival, and the labor movement, see Deborah S. Bernstein, ed., *Pioneers and Homemakers: Jewish Women in Pre-State Israel* (Albany: State University of New York Press, 1992).

20. For a discussion of Chemda Ben-Yehuda's life and work, see Nurit Govrin, *Honey from a Rock* [Hebrew] (Tel Aviv: Misrad habitachon, 1989), 45–52.

21. Nechama Feinstein-Pukhachevski, "74 Questions of the Daughters" [1889], in Govrin, *The First Half*, 132–133.

22. Eliezer Ben-Yehuda, "On Women and Hebrew" [Hebrew]; reprinted in Govrin, *Honey from a Rock*, 53.

23. It was not until the twenties that a generation of Hebrew-speaking women arose who had not encountered Hebrew from the wrong side of the mechitsa, as it were, but who had learned it as another language. The women poets of the Third Aliya were, in fact, successful at turning the Hebrew literary idiom into the flexible expressive instrument, outside of what Alter has called the "echo chamber" of Hebrew literary tradition. Poets like Esther Raab, arguably the first native Hebrew poet, and Rachel, who wrote a Hebrew as simple and distilled as the Russian Acmeist poets who were her influences, enacted the Hebrew modernist revolution Shlonsky called for but was unable to fully bring to fruition in his own work (his manifesto against allusion is, perhaps with conscious irony, itself a "tissue of quotations"), nor did he truly recognize it when he saw it. Nevertheless, the new generation of Hebrew women poets was never accepted as fully into the canon as the Yiddish women poets who arose during the same decade. See Michael Gluzman, "Suppressed Modernisms: Marginality, Politics, Canon Formation" (Ph.D. dissertation, University of California, Berkeley, 1993), 37–100.

24. Rachel Katznelson-Shazar, *The Person as He-She Was* [Hebrew], ed. Michal Hagiti (Tel Aviv: Am Oved, [1962] 1989), quoted from a 1931 entry in Katznelson-Shazar's diary, pp. 329–330.

25. Y. Avineri, "On Ze'ev Jabotinsky," in *Ze'ev Jabotinsky: On the Twentieth*

Anniversary of His Death [Hebrew] (Tel Aviv: Hamashbir Hamercazi Press, 1961), 316–328.

26. *Zev Jabotinsky* [Hebrew] (Jerusalem: Hebrew Language Academy, 1970), 7.

27. Zrubavel, "We Accuse and Demand Responsibility" [Yiddish], in *Journal of the League for the Rights of Yiddish in the Land of Israel* (1936), 17–18, quoted in *Never Say Die*, 297–312. Zrubavel, a left-wing Labor Zionist who continued to champion Yiddish while living in Palestine, fought this and other similar anti-Yiddish policies.

28. Alter Druyanov, *The Book of Jokes and Witticisms* [Hebrew] (Tel Aviv: Dvir Press, [1945] 1991), joke no. 2663.

29. Ben-Yehuda, *The Dream and Its Fulfillment*, 205.

30. Harshav, *Language in Time of Revolution*, 163.

31. Ze'ev Jabotinsky, the letter of 6 Adar 1927, *Jabotinsky's Letters* [Hebrew] (Tel Aviv: Merkaz Press, 1972).

32. For an analysis of Israeli Hebrew speech patterns, see Tamar Katriel, *Talking Straight: Dugri Speech in Israeli Sabra Culture* (New York and Cambridge: Cambridge University Press, 1986).

33. Itamar Even-Zohar quotes from Druyanov's collection *Jokes and Witticisms* (Hebrew), in "Language Conflict and National Identity," in *Nationalism and Modernity: A Mediterranean Perspective*, ed. Joseph Alpher (Haifa: University of Haifa, 1986), 131–132.

34. Yehoash, *Ketuvim* (1 May 1929).

35. Even-Zohar, "Language Conflict and National Identity," 132.

36. Yeshurun Keshet, "The Works of Dvora Baron" [Hebrew], in *Dvora Baron: A Selection of Critical Essays on Her Work*, ed. Ada Pagis (Tel Aviv: Am Oved Press, 1974), 120.

37. This incident is discussed in Arye Pilovski, *Between Yes and No: Yiddish and Yiddish Literature in Erets-Israel, 1907–1948* [Yiddish] (Tel Aviv: World Council for Yiddish and Jewish Culture, 1986), 213–215.

38. Pilovski, *Between Yes and No*, 214, cites a letter written originally to the Hebrew daily *Do'ar hayom* and reprinted in the Yiddish journal *Literarishe bleter* in which L. Chayn-Shimoni described the incident as a "pogrom."

39. Cited in Pilovski, *Between Yes and No*, 213.

40. Michael Berkowitz, *Zionist Culture and West European Jewry before the First World War* (Cambridge: Cambridge University Press, 1993), 19.

41. Max Nordau, "*Muskeljudentum*," *Juedische Turnzeitung* (June 1903), reprinted as "Muscular Judaism," trans. J. Hessing, in *The Jew in the Modern World*, ed. Paul Mendes-Flohr (New York and Oxford: Oxford University Press, 1980), 435.

42. Elon, *The Israelis*, 120.

43. Ilana Pardes, "The Poetic Strength of a Matronym," in *Gender and Text in Modern Hebrew and Yiddish Literature*, ed. Naomi B. Sokoloff, Anne Lapidos Lerner, and Anita Norich (New York: Jewish Theological Seminary, 1992), 41–42.

44. For more on Bat-Chama, see Dan Miron's *Founding Mothers, Stepsisters* [Hebrew] (Tel Aviv: Hakibuts Hame'uchad Press, 1991), 13, 38–42.

45. *Working Women's Word* [Hebrew], ed. Rachel Katznelson-Shazar (Tel-Aviv: Mo'etset hapo'alot, 1930), i–iii.

46. Chayim Nagid, "An Interview with the Poet Avot Yeshurun" [Hebrew], *Yediyot Achronot* (11 October 1974).

47. Isaac Leyb Peretz, "Introductory Remarks" [Yiddish], in *The First Yiddish Language Conference* (Vilna, 1931), 66.

48. Sholem Ash, "Resolution" [Yiddish], in *The First Yiddish Language Conference*, 82.

49. Katznelson-Shazar, "Language Wanderings," 192. This passage does not appear in the Yiddish translation.

50. Ibid., 192–193.

51. Amos Elon, *Herzl* (New York: Holt, Rinehart and Winston, 1975), 245.

52. Yankev Glatshteyn, "There Where the Cedars" [Yiddish], in *Credos* (New York: Verlag Yiddish Leben, 1929), 72.

53. Janet Hadda, *Yankev Glatshteyn* (Boston: Twayne Publishers, 1980), 140–141.

54. Achad Ha'am, "The Way of the Spirit" [Hebrew], *At a Crossroad*, vol. 2 (Dvir: Tel Aviv, [1898] 1961), 111.

55. "A Reception for Ash and Hirshbein" [Hebrew], *Ketuvim* (18 May 1927), 1.

56. Avraham Shlonsky, "On 'Peace' " [Hebrew], *Ketuvim* (18 May 1927), 1.

57. See the chapter entitled "Zionism as an Erotic Revolution," in David Biale, *Eros and the Jews: From Biblical Israel to Contemporary America* (New York: Basic Books, 1992).

58. Avraham Shlonsky, "Freshness" [Hebrew] (1923), reprinted in *The Successors of Symbolism in Poetry*, ed. Benjamin Hrushovski (Jerusalem: Akademon, 1973), 153.

59. Avraham Shlonsky, "Poesy" [Hebrew], "Hump of the World" (1922), reprinted in *The Successors of Symbolism in Poetry*, 154.

60. Zohar Shavit, *Literary Life in Palestine: 1910–1933* [Hebrew] (Tel Aviv: Hakibuts Hame'uchad Press, 1982), 176–177.

61. Uri-Tsvi Greenberg, *The Complete Works* [Hebrew] (Jerusalem: Mosad Bialik, 1990), 82.

62. Ibid., 85.

63. Uri-Tsvi Greenberg, *To the Ninety Nine* [Hebrew] (Tel Aviv: Sadan Press, 1928), 15.

64. Ibid., 20.

65. Katznelson-Shazar, "Language Wanderings," 235–236.

Index

Compositor:	J. Jarrett Engineering, Inc.
Text:	10/13 Aldus
Display:	Aldus
Printer:	Thomson-Shore
Binder:	Thomson-Shore